Prayer in Action

To Sister Aletha with the hope
that you will continue to realize
in your own life the true
meaning of prayer: "to rest in
Him as He works in you" From

Sister Marian

September 13, 1980

Prayer in Action:
A Growth Experience

Miriam Murphy

Abingdon
Nashville

PRAYER IN ACTION: A GROWTH EXPERIENCE

Copyright © 1979 by Abingdon

Library of Congress Cataloging in Publication Data

MURPHY, MIRIAM.
   Prayer in action.
   Bibliography: p.
   1. Prayer. 2. Spiritual life—Catholic authors.
I. Title.
BV215.M86   248'.3   79-983

ISBN 0-687-33372-5

Scripture quotations unless otherwise noted are based on the Revised Standard
Version of the Bible, copyright 1946, 1952, © 1971, 1973 by the Division of
Christian Education of the National Council of Churches of Christ in the
U.S.A.

Scripture quotations noted GNB are from Today's English Version of the Bible
(Good News for Modern Man). Copyright © American Bible Society 1966,
1971, 1976.

Scripture quotations noted KJV are from the King James Version of the Bible.

MANUFACTURED BY THE PARTHENON PRESS
NASHVILLE, TENNESSEE, UNITED STATES OF AMERICA

To Mary, the first sanctuary of Jesus; a model for the maturing Christian growing in an intimate relationship with Christ while sharing him with others—through suffering to glory.

Contents

Part 3
Fostering Maturity

Foreword

When I first met Sister Miriam Murphy—over lunch at the Nassau Club in the Spring of 1977—I was already predisposed in her favor. I have always been in considerable awe (and envy) of a person able to make a total commitment of life in a religious order.

I was fascinated to discover in that first meeting that we were on the same wavelength in our assessment of the religious mood of the nation. She articulated what Gallup Poll figures seemed to be saying about the spiritual climate of the nation: that Americans are earnestly groping for a spiritual base for their lives.

Many Americans report they have had profound religious experiences, but do they find the spiritual food they need in organized religion? A recent survey we conducted for a group of thirty-one religious denominations (convened by the National Council of Churches of Christ) shows that large percentages, both inside and outside organized religion, accuse churches of losing their "spiritual character."

The results of this survey suggest, I believe, that churches may be ill-prepared to deal with spiritual experiences. What appears to be called for is a "spiritual ministry" to insure that the church would communicate with people who are all charged up about their faith, but who currently feel spiritually homeless. So I was pleased to find that while Sister Miriam was obviously a very spiritual person, she was also a pragmatist. She immediately saw an important contribution that scientific surveys of public opinion can make to our understanding of religious climate of the nation. In this respect she was ahead of many religious leaders who have been slow to come to the view that surveys, if properly conducted, can provide valuable indicators for the study of the spiritual climate of our time.

Our commonality of interests, incidentally, soon led to the formation of the Princeton Religion Research Center, the purpose of which is to gain a better understanding of the nature and depth of religious commitment in the United States and abroad and to explore ways this information can enable leaders to promote spiritual growth.

I also discovered in that first meeting—and again it was a happy discovery—that Sister Miriam, while sharply critical of the extravagances and pretentions of certain religious movements, did not let her feelings keep her from noting the good and positive elements of these movements. In fact, she is eager to identify and strengthen the commonalities among the various faiths and denominations. She is a thorough-going ecumenist.

Sister Miriam reminds us in this book that bingo, potluck suppers, and committee meetings have little to do with true religion—that what is really needed is not *communication* among people, but *communion*—communion rooted in love of Christ.

She warns us not to be caught up in pseudo-religious movements where the central focus is not God, but a contemporary human being or one's self. The touchstone, she says, is not "how great I am" but "how great thou art."

Sister Miriam fully appreciates the importance of the "born again" experience as an initial awakening (she believes it is akin to what Teresa of Avila called infused contemplation), but she reminds us that we must not be too caught up with adulation about "the day I found Christ" and forget about "the day after."

It could be said of the American people that they are in a period of spiritual adolescence, eagerly and impulsively groping for the means by which to live out their faith. In surveys we find that Americans indeed have a strong will to believe, and many say they have "felt the presence of God." Furthermore, as high a proportion as six in ten say they have "made a commitment to Jesus Christ."

But it is, of course, abundantly clear that most of us encounter great difficulty in living our faith in a consistent manner. We also forget that it is as necessary to grow spiritually as intellectually. A form of spiritual growth in a perfect blending of prayer in action is undoubtedly attainable. This is the message of Sister Miriam Murphy's book.

I believe it speaks directly to the spiritual needs of the times and to non-Christians as well as Christians. *Prayer in Action* is clearly written and will speak to scholars and lay persons alike.

Sister Miriam guides us through the difficult shoals in our spiritual life and ends her book with how to foster maturity through prayer in view of personal and social renewal.

Sister Miriam has been thorough in her search for the positive elements of various religious faiths and movements in this country and has brought a broad range of academic and personal experience to this search. She has taken very seriously the biblical injunction, "Put all things to the test and keep what is good" (I Thess. 5:21).

George Gallup, Jr.

Introduction

(The comments in this and the following chapter do not concern the heart of prayer in action; however, I think it is important for the reader to understand what prompted me to write this book and to give some of the live sources of my information.)

The untimely death of Thomas Merton in the Orient called world-wide attention to his desire to understand the "new" religious consciousness, at a time when Oriental cults were gaining momentum in the West. His quest is a reminder to Christians today of our duty to "put all things to the test and keep what is good" (I Thess. 5:21).

Merton did not limit his search in the area of religious consciousness to Eastern religious movements. Before his death in 1968, he had already begun writing about the then emerging neo-Pentecostalism and as Dr. A. R. Arazteh, a transpersonal psychologist, told me in a phone interview, Merton had visited him prior to his departure for the Orient to seek further insight into transpersonal psychology, that fourth and newest psychological school which emphasizes the development of a person's fullest potential in all aspects of his sensory, psychic, *and* spiritual well-being.

The challenge to understand the new religious consciousness is even greater today than at the time of Merton's death. Gallup figures point out that at least six million Americans are involved in Transcendental Meditation, four million in Yoga, three million in mysticism, and one million in Eastern religions.

Moreover, increasing numbers are becoming involved in inner healing and physical healing, and pseudo-psychic religious cults. The charismatic renewal, once called the neo-Pentecostal movement, now is thriving with three million devotees.

It occurred to me a few years ago, that if someone so well-versed in Christian spirituality as Merton, in fact the foremost contemporary spokesman, whose books on contemplation have been bestsellers for a quarter of a century, saw fit to probe the new religious consciousness, how much more the rest of us?

This became apparent to me shortly after Vatican II when I became heavily involved in interfaith relations in Columbus, Ohio, and was endeavoring to realize the vision of John XXIII to build bridges of goodwill and Christian understanding. As I look back, I am amazed how communication between Protestants and Catholics has improved in so short a time. I now smile at those early stilted efforts to initiate the process through "Living Room Dialogues," those miniature headtrips on topics of common concern, undergirded with such delicate reminders in the handbook that there indeed are saints and sinners, mature and immature Christians in all denominations; should we not refrain from referral to the worst stereotypes of other Christians? Today, the warm spontaneous relationships found in many interfaith prayer groups are in marked contrast to these early awkward efforts.

One thing led to another and I was invited regularly to speak at formal and informal Protestant gatherings, my favorite topic being the changing nun. Every time I gave it I had to change it, changes were occurring so fast! And as I milled around in the Protestant community I found myself learning while sharing. What an inspiration to find so many deeply "spiritual" Protestants; I soon had friends with a commitment to prayer among Evangelicals, Baptists, and Methodists akin to what might be found in a Catholic religious order. I was especially impressed by the richness and diversity among Christian denominations, which seemed comparable to the many ways of life in Catholic religious communities. As a matter of fact, I began to compare Presbyterians with their emphasis on order and intellectual attainment to Jesuits; Episcopalians with their stress on the refinements of worship to Benedictines; and Methodists with their interest in the poor and downtrodden to Franciscans. It was astonishing to find that while Catholics were shedding their legalisms and in a sense becoming "de-Romanized," Protestants, with heavy emphasis on structure and procedure, were highly "Romanized." I could go on and on. Needless to say, besides sharing I was learning and really enjoying myself when quite unexpectedly another challenge surfaced, a challenge to understand the new religious consciousness about which I knew very little. I could understand how Merton must have felt before departing for the Orient. There was something out there I needed to know about, and I felt a responsibility to understand what was going on.

One of many occurrences which brought this about was a conversation with Lola and Gene who were much involved with reincarnation and who persistently cross-questioned me on the subject. Without too much ado I simply called attention to what appeared to me to be shortsightedness and immaturity. After all, Christianity as an Eastern religion, I observed, had an approach to reincarnation beyond which we cannot go since each Christian has a sublime calling to allow Christ to grow within. This, I remarked, is the great "reincarnational" mystery of Christianity first experienced by Mary which continues to be experienced by us today in a deep but real way. "Why putter around," I remarked, "with being the reincarnation of some medieval knight or lady?" They had no answer. By then, too, my insights on the subject were exhausted!

As time went on, however, I began to see the need to fill in the gaps in my own understandings of the new religious consciousness. I had heard about young people turning from drugs to Jesus, of executives and football players going in for Transcendental Meditation, of friends in the then "neo-Pentecostal" prayer meetings, of acquaintances taking up

Yoga, of others being helped at healing services, but I had no first-hand knowledge of these developments so I began to ask myself, Was there something in all this which I as a nun should know about that would enrich my own spiritual life and stimulate further growth and maturity? Was there something I should know about which would make me more effective in my outreach and interfaith role? My life as a nun had given me a firm grip on the inner life under the guidance of a spiritual director who had taught me much about the Christian spirituality of John of the Cross and Teresa of Avila. I had discovered too, the depths of Christian consciousness to be found in scripture.

At that point I simply took advantage of every opportunity that came my way, and I launched on an exploratory period, a "probe unlimited"! I responded, for instance, to an invitation to a seminar at Oral Roberts University where I interviewed Bob Stamps, Charles Farah, and Howard Irwin on the faculty there; I had a lengthy interview with the well-known Swami Satchindinada on a plane from Columbus to New York and gleaned insights on Yoga which I never could have gotten from books. To my surprise I found he knew more about the Christian spiritual classics than some nuns and priests, not to say Protestant clergy. I also had a conversation with Morton Kelsey, a well-known Jungian psychologist on demonology, when he lectured at a Presbyterian church in Columbus. I interviewed the world-renowned Pentecostal authority Walter Hollenweger, Professor of Theology at the University of Birmingham, England, while he was giving a series of lectures at Capitol University in Columbus. At the same time I interviewed Dr. John Mackay, President Emeritus of Princeton Theological Seminary, an architect of the Presbyterian policy statement on the charismatic renewal and author of *Christian Reality and Appearance.* I also lunched with William Johnston, S. J., a writer with twenty-five years of scholarship on Zen and author of *Silent Music* and *The Still Point,* when he was giving a retreat. I might add that my unlimited probe also included some

planned interviews and other scheduled events such as
interviews with: Krister Stendahl, Dean of Harvard Divinity
School on the new religious movements seen in historic
perspective; George Maloney, S.J., a prolific writer on
contemporary Eastern Christian spirituality who lives what he
writes; David DuPlessis, world-renowned Pentecostal ecumenist; A. R. Arazteh, transpersonal psychologist; Rodman
Williams, president of the Charismatic Ecumenical Institute at
Anaheim, California.

I also attended lectures, workshops, and religious meetings
of all varieties. For instance, there was the lecture, "The
Out-of-Body Experience," a workshop on demonology with
Don Basham, a lecture on Bio-Feedback followed by a testing
of states of relaxation with the use of Bio-Feedback apparatus. I
participated in a "Pastoral Care Institute" with sessions on
inner healing and visited a Yoga Ashram; I went to meetings on
Transcendental Meditation and psychic healing. On the
grassroots level, I interviewed Hare Krishna and Moon
devotees in the O'Hare and Pittsburg airports, and talked with
three persons who claimed to have had a vision of Christ: one
the wife of a professor, another a maintenance man, and the
third a Lutheran pastor. I interviewed those who had had
dramatic, medically confirmed healings at Leroy Jenkins
Crusades and Kathryn Kuhlman meetings.

My own participation and involvement included attending
numerous neo-Pentecostal prayer meetings in various regions
and localities, it meant being the recipient of inner and physical
healings, as well as ministering to others. I used the Christian
mantra, the Jesus Prayer, taught to me by George Maloney,
continuing to meditate as I had done for years in much the same
way as those in some meditation groups were starting to do. I
finally began to wonder whether I had gone beyond the call of
duty and was reminded of what Merton wrote in his Asian diary
dated November 18, 1968. He said he had come to realize that
the East held nothing for him he could not have found or did not

already have in his own tradition and vocation as a monk and hermit of the West.

Little by little my conviction concerning the need for an *understanding* the new consciousness and its bearing on Christian maturity grew. But why should I or anyone else, for that matter, want to probe in this area? I found my answer in Colossians:

> We ask God to fill you with all the *understanding* that his Spirit gives. Then you will be able to *live* as the Lord wants and will always *do* what pleases him. Your lives will be fruitful in all kinds of good works and you will grow in your knowledge of God. (1:9-10 *italics added*)

I had come a long way in putting many things to the test and keeping what was good. Now, as I looked to the future, I could envision vast numbers in the vanguard of the Christianity of the future. Those people who today will only come to—or back to—Christianity through the entrance of transcendence are destined to bring vitality to the Christian churches to the glory of God in time and in eternity. For this vision of the future to come to life a new ministry is needed, a ministry that understands, nurtures, and fosters maturity.

PART ONE
UNDERSTANDING MATURITY

Chapter I
Put All Things to the Test

My First Awakening

The scope and complexity of the new religious consciousness had not occurred to me when I first launched on my probe unlimited. It was only after I got into it that I had a powerful awakening. Then I began to ask myself: "Is it possible to understand this new religious consciousness from Pentecostalism to Zen in a way that would be tailored to my beliefs as a Christian?" However, I did realize to some extent the complexity of my search since I had already spent considerable time learning about neo-Pentecostalism; neo-Orientalism; Sufism; Tibetan Buddhism; psychic, physical, and inner healing, Transcendental Meditation; the Hare Krishna Movement; Reincarnation; as well as the Divine Light Mission; the Maharashi Mahesh Yoga; Transpersonal Psychology; clairvoyance; extrasensory perception, precognition, retrocognition, telepathy; and levitation! The need for my probe unlimited to become a limited probe was quite apparent.

My sympathy went out to pastors when I found myself becoming an interfaith sounding board for disgruntled Christians who complained that their pastors' lack of insight and ministry to the new religious consciousness left much to be desired. He was simply "not with it." The following comment from *Christian Ministry* sums up the situation as I saw it at the time:

The contemplative life is back in fashion these days. Add to that the fact that the many Eastern religions, with their almost quietistic approach to life, hold a deep fascination for many Christians. Mix in the discoveries in the fields of psychiatry and psychology. Drop in a flavoring of demonology, a bit of hypnotism, and scenes from current movies and best sellers. The resulting mix is truly a brew sure to befuddle the average person not to mention the pastor who must deal with parishioners whose old certainties have been shaken.[1]

Before proceeding further, I stood back and took a look at the situation. Perhaps the simplest way to resolve the complexity was to limit the probe. Instead of attempting to analyse religious consciousness from Pentecostalism to Zen I had to get a hold on religious consciousness as it relates to natural consciousness. So I did. I discovered that the "new" religious consciousness is as old as humanity. It is that part of our natural consciousness which is likely to get lost in a civilization as rationalistic and legalistic as that bequeathed to us by the Romans. I also discovered that it is likely to appear during movements of renewal in the church or in situations where it has been neglected for some time. This is one way we can explain the upsurge of interest today in spiritual consciousness.

I also recalled my college theology classes and the classic proofs for the existence of God. Among them was the fact that all people of all time have acknowledged God's existence. It had not occurred to me that this conviction, imbedded deep within the human psyche, is a form of natural consciousness. In fact, as a natural endowment it provides a common base for belief among all denominations and all religions. Religious breakthroughs into levels of expanded consciousness have been referred to in many ways:

Zen Buddhism	Satori
Yoga	Samadi or Maksha
Taoism	The Absolute Tao
Sufism	Fani

Martin Buber   the I-Thou relationship
Abraham Maslow   the peak experience
Rudolf Otto   the numinous

Peak experiences in Christian consciousness also have their special terminologies which, as we will see later, mean something quite different from other forms of religious consciousness. The following are the more familiar Christian expressions:

Teresa of Avila, the "Seventh Mansion"
John of the Cross, the "Living Flame"
Teilhard de Chardin, the "Omega Point"

As I was reflecting on all this it became clear that religious consciousness, which is beyond sensations, images, and abstract thinking, can go in any direction. Just as our vocal chords can assist us in the rendition of a hymn or of rock'n'roll, human consciousness can be an instrument for black magic or under the gentle guidance of the Holy Spirit, bringing us to the highest reaches of consciousness known to humanity—communion with God.

The Limited Probe

I was beginning to realize that by narrowing the probe still further to a more intensive concentration on Christian consciousness per se I would be right on target; that is, if we have a grasp of the essence and meaning of Christian consciousness, we can evaluate everything else in terms of its central focus. Certainly, the numberless people and variety of beliefs that crossed my path impressed the importance of this focus on me. For instance, there was a judge, my first encounter with an anti-intellectual, a neo-Pentecostal of the old type, who was completely hung up on religious phenomena and his four Bible quotes, with no appreciation whatsoever of the inner healing, renewing power of the Holy Spirit within. There were Ph.D's with a third-grade knowledge of religion who were attentive listeners at a lecture "How to Have an Out-of-Body Experience" (in three easy lessons)—conducted by an off-focus clergyman who never once mentioned the saving love of Christ within. There was the heart specialist enthusiastic over new meditation techniques based on "selfist" psychology—only too likely to provide a heart attack for the unconverted sinner caught up in his own dross without Christ in him to help him out. As I reflected on all this, I began to feel a mission to those "out there," those who were sincere, searching, and growing without benefit of ministry of any sort. How could I have the crassness, however, to even think that what I had to write would make that much difference? Later I realized that much of what I had to say needed to be written. So I decided to keep going, knowing I could at least hope to trigger further response and writing on the part of other readers.

A book by Dr. John Mackay, President Emeritus of Princeton Theological Seminary, called *Christian Reality and Appearance* influenced me also. It has a strong interfaith message encouraging Christians of all denominations to focus on the central reality of Christianity, an experience as well as a fact, namely, a relationship with Jesus Christ. We should see all else in our church life, important though it seems, says Mackay, as mere shadows of this reality. I began to view the Christian life as the experience of growing in this relationship from communication to communion with God and fellow people which included a "Christian consciousness," i.e., an awareness of God's personal love, given through the redemptive power of Christ, acting on the human consciousness, while becoming the energizing force in an activated faith.

The complexity of the initial stage of probing had now been completely resolved. Unfortunately, though, I then acquired other problems leading me from complexity to perplexity.

This happened about the time I became a visiting scholar at
Princeton Theological Seminary, where Dr. Jack Cooper,
Director of the Center of Continuing Education, gave me an
endless amount of support and encouragement. But I ran into
difficulty poring over hundreds of volumes at the outstanding
Speer Library, when I discovered I was working in an area in
which there had been very little recent scholarship.

I was perplexed when I soon came to realize that the lack of
attention by scholars in the past century to Christianity as an
experience was reflected in the dearth of available resources. I
found all the well-known spiritual classics by Poulain,
Underhill, von Heugel, William James, Rudolf Otto, and
others; some were too esoteric to make the average reader
stop and listen. Then there were anthologies on religious
consciousness also of little use to the modern reader,
inasmuch as they take us in one leap to the middle of an
exalted experience or state of religious consciousness with no
previous information as to how one gets there. Such works are
not too helpful to modern Christians in their attempts to
understand Christian consciousness. Then there were, of
course, those writings on Christian consciousness, as related
to the maturing process, of Teresa of Avila and John of the
Cross. These works, with their strong biblical undergirdings,
are among the greatest classics of their kind. But they lack
up-dated commentaries because scholars are only now
starting to refine translations of these masterpieces. Most of
the material for which I was looking was simply nonexistent.
When a Princeton professor asked me out of the blue one day
for a bibliography in the area of Christian consciousness, I felt
affirmed in my conclusion, since apparently he had been
looking too. I was again affirmed by a comment of Martin
Marty's that Christians by and large have allowed their rich
resources in the area of religious experience to atrophy. Until
recently though, who would have given a second thought to
the matter? The books I checked out from the library

indicated I was the second reader, the first having been five years before!

Besides the lack of up-dated material, another matter perplexed me now, one which would have a direct bearing on my writing: the possible difficulty of interfaith communication on the subject of Christian consciousness. How could I write in a way that would be heard, without attempting to start a whole new school of theology or design a whole new vocabulary? Paul Tillich once said that to be able to communicate on matters of general agreement, Christians would have to devise a new vocabulary. I was not about to do this, I planned to merely confine myself to recording a few insights and reflections. However, an experience I had had a short time before left an indelible impression. I was invited to address the staff of Scripture Press at Wheaton, Illinois, a stronghold of Protestant conservatism. Never having met a Protestant fundamentalist in my life, I talked away blithely and confidently on the changing nun and then called for questions. The first was not long in coming. "Have you had the born-again experience?" My horrifying response: "What do *you* mean by that?" I was instantly rejoined with: *"YOU* mean you do not know the meaning of a born-again experience . . . have never heard of Nicodemus?" "That isn't what I said," I replied; "If you tell me what *you* mean by the born-again experience, then I will tell you whether I have had the experience you are talking about."

The effect was like the debate Paul precipitated when he brought up the question of resurrection while on trial before the Pharisees and Sadducees. The staff forgot all about me and for a moment began to argue among themselves. As a Catholic nun this was a complete revelation to me. Here was a central belief to which they were all committed yet they did not seem to be in accord as to what it actually meant. Finally, after much back and forth among themselves, they came to an ad-hoc agreement by pooling their components of the born-again experience. They told me what they meant, and without hesitation, I immediately responded: Yes, of course I have had the born-again experience. When I committed my life to Christ, as a nun and became his witness, I had what Teresa of Avila calls "a touch of infused contemplation."

At that moment there was virtual pandemonium: pencils dropped on their pads, eyebrows were raised, mouths opened, and audible signs of dismay were heard about the room. What on earth was "infused contemplation"? I heard several mutter. I didn't realize at the time exactly what I had done that was wrong, but I knew it wasn't right. The chairman closed the meeting. I had not scored a victory, but I had had one beautiful lesson: the lack of communication among Christians committed to a realization of Christ's love and presence and a deepening relationship with him. As I look back on the incident, I wonder what would have happened had I become more articulate and attempted to communicate by further explaining my understanding of Christ-consciousness in the obsolete terminology of classic Christian writers; or had I moved to the matter of "receiving" Christ defined in my terms of receiving Christ daily in Holy Communion. As I recall this memorable experience at Wheaton, knowing that today a professor is there who is working on improved relationships and communication between Roman Catholics and mainline Christians, I experience a "strange warmth" in Wesley's words.

I had the Wheaton incident on my mind and was feeling perplexed about moving ahead in my writing and research, but the challenge of awakening an interest in a better understanding and expression of Christian consciousness for the sake of fostering a more mature Christianity today was too great. I decided to take the risk, perplexity or no perplexity.

My Second Awakening

So in spite of the perplexities raised by a dearth of resources, as well as problems of interfaith communication, I made up my mind to stay with my mission and ferret out the difficulties involved in refining the probe. It was only then that I realized something was missing. Was I really getting at the heart of the matter, or was I on a headtrip? Presently I had another awakening: Of what value was it to *understand* the new Christian consciousness without carefully observing its effect on mature Christians? I found there were two ways of looking at this: First, I discovered that some Christians do not normally associate religious experience with Christianity in any serious way. And second, those who do, generally identify religious experience with immaturity.

Upon researching the first reaction, I learned that Christianity in the understanding of the early Christians was more than a creed, a code, or a form of worship. It was an experience of a living reality in an altered state of consciousness, a Christian consciousness. Dionysius wrote of a certain early Christian; "Hierotheus is perfect in divine things because he not only learns them, he experiences them." The Holy Spirit through the gift of wisdom gives us the power to experience divine things, to taste them in the depths of our being, and then through this divine experience to judge all things.

The second reaction was more obvious to me since I had personally witnessed the effervescent enthusiasm of some beginners—those who cheer for Jesus but seldom regard Jesus as the *Still* Point—which often turns off the mainline churchgoer. In fact, I confess, I used poor taste once when I addressed a neo-Pentecostal group and entitled my talk "Pentecostal Noise or Poise!" Something told me, however, that there was more behind this surface emotionalism than meets the eye and, as Krister Stendahl suggests, that "high voltage" is needed today to recharge the church.

While poring over a book by Donald Bloesch, I was fascinated by an insight which shed light on the historic reason for the association of emotionalism with immaturity.

The question which really bothered me, however, was not so much the emotionalism as the continual emphasis on initial

awakenings and beginnings with which emotionalism is often
associated. For me, Donald Bloesch, in "Essentials of
Evangelical Theology," seems to throw light on the reason for
this repeated emphasis on beginnings. He claims that both
Luther and Calvin had a doctrine of sanctification but that
both men only sounded the call to repentence and neglected
on-going sanctification; not because they did not believe in it,
but because the tragic circumstances of their time prevented
them from developing their theology further. Undoubtedly,
this is one underlying cause for the emotional and flamboyant
witnessing to an initial experience in early American
revivalism. The theology of that day stressed the sudden event
rather than the gradual transformation of personality through
a whole lifetime of conversion, redirection, and sustained
support, as Christians shared with one another the grace of
Christ's triumph. While the emotionalism has calmed down
somewhat, the remnants of an instant, complete-holiness
concept following an initial awakening is not uncommon
today.

Christian consciousness as something beyond an initial
awakening stage, or as it relates to the maturing process, was
also totally neglected in post-Reformation theology. The
emphasis seemed to be more on a holy gospel rather than a
holy people. As far as I was concerned Bloesch's historical
view made a lot of sense because I had been trying to figure out
why so much attention was given to those initial awakening
experiences—the "day I found Christ"—with no mention of
the "day after." It told me, too, why understanding in the
minds of many with regard to Christian consciousness is
limited to the dramatic awakening rather than the deep peace
of Christ in the depths of the human psyche.

As I was reflecting on all of this and putting some aspects of
my observations to the test, I began to realize that the
immaturity of the guru worshipers and the egocentric
meditators went deeper than that of the exuberant neo-
Pentecostals. It was really a matter of focus which made the

difference, not surface emotionalism. The former, in their optimistic view of human nature, are forfeiting their freedom in and through Christ when they dispense with a personal relationship with him, while, ideally speaking, the latter are on the path to maturity because of their focus on the Reality within because of their reverence for Christ as they seek to make him their Lord.

By now I was nearing the end of my probe. I had already decided in spite of foreseen difficulties to explore "What is the essence of Christian consciousness?" And I was convinced that Christian consciousness, as it related to a mature Christian life-style, was also a matter for further consideration.

Yet another question was persistently surfacing. Why is there a need to be concerned about these questions at all? Once more I examined some recent Gallup figures and learned that Gallup surveys show that there is not only a widespread interest today in nonmaterial values, but also an awareness of the need to grow spiritually, a desire to cultivate a deep inner life, and a strong inclination to integrate a life of prayer with service. Moreover, as I reviewed the study on the churched and unchurched American, I discovered that both churched and unchurched responded affirmatively, and in sizeable numbers, that for them the church had lost its spiritual meaning. Six in ten among the unchurched and as many as one half of the churched agreed strongly or moderately on this issue. When asked if most churches or synagogues were too concerned with organizational as opposed to spiritual issues, 47 percent of the churched and 56 percent of the unchurched said yes.

While these figures need further probing and analysis, they do suggest that there are Christians around who are looking to Christian churches for more spiritual leadership than they are now actually receiving. A clear proof of this is to be found in the fact that of the numbers involved in religious consciousness movements, seven in ten are *already* church members!

This raises a simple question. If they are completely satisfied with the depth of ministry being provided by the churches, why are they looking elsewhere? Among the churchgoers there are 43 percent who report having had a religious experience and 24 percent among the unchurched.

There is no comparable statistical evidence that Christian churches by and large, other than token retreats, occasional healing services, and a lecture or two, are doing much to meet the massive need of those who are hungry for the transcendent. Many are groping for growth, so that any effort to help them to better understand Christian consciousness in contrast with other forms is vitally necessary. All of us, regardless of denomination, are in need of this understanding so that we will be able to live as the Lord wants and to do what pleases him (Col. 1:9). We need the kind of understanding for which Merton was searching—the insight and wisdom for which he paid a great price.

What the situation today actually demands is a new form of ministry—a ministry for maturity—a unique form of evangelism not merely for those already called to commitment but a call of all to maturity. A ministry to the hungry and thirsty, to those beginning to experience a Christian consciousness and a relationship with Christ within. A ministry to those who are in need of a deeper understanding of the spiritual treasures hidden in the field. A ministry of counseling, instruction, and encouragement as Christians grow in their deepening relationship with the risen Lord.

Is there something we as Christians could do to understand, nurture, and foster the process of maturity among Christians everywhere? How can we bridge the gaps in our understandings so that we can more readily assume our responsibilities to foster a mature Christianity, as well as meet the common threat to authentic Christianity lurking in many of the new "consciousness" trends? Certainly, Christianity has always been a haven for sinners, but the Christian church was never meant to be homogeneous in this respect! Each church community needs a few more mature Christians, those clearly growing toward the full stature of Christ. This should be our common cause. And we should generously share our saints with one another, particularly those endowed with special gifts for the church at large. Interfaith collaboration in fostering maturity in relation to Christian consciousness should be given serious consideration as a future undertaking.

The ministry for maturity brings us back to our common roots and reminds us that it was only *after* the early Christians had a personal awareness and consciousness of Christ that they were brought to a deeper understanding of Christian consciousness and of how it relates to an on-going Christian life-style. They then received instruction and catechesis which enabled them to mature in him. A ministry for maturity should encourage those with a Christian consciousness to mature until they reach the very height of Christ's full stature (Eph. 4:13). This process begins with informal counseling and instruction in the various aspects of the life of the new Christian, as we are reminded in words of Paul: "We teach everyone . . . in order to bring each one into God's presence as a *mature* individual in union with Christ" (Col. 1:28). To begin with we must understand more fully what Christian maturity is in relation to Christian consciousness.

Chapter II
Christian Maturity:
The Call of All

Christian Consciousness and Christian Maturity

Christian maturity is a call to all. A call expressed in John: "He who abides in him should walk as he walked." We need to "keep the seal of baptism shining" as expressed in ancient Christian documents and inscriptions. Christian maturity is an inner process of being perfected by the indwelling God. It is a growing, deepening relationship with Father, Son, and Holy Spirit, which in some mysterious and unique way often reaches the level of consciousness.

Some will argue that there is little evidence that Christian consciousness has much bearing on a mature Christian life-style. How is it, they will insist, that those who talk the most about their Jesus experiences give little evidence of observing his precepts and counsels? They point to the remarkable immaturity of those ardent Christians with that clean-washed look who have a charismatic glow and enthusiastic smile, yet when all is said and done, there is more said than done. These critics, however, judge Christian maturity solely on the basis of appearance, performance, and moral perfection.

In retrospect, there is no reason to suppose that those early Christians who experienced Christ were more virtuous than some who experience him today. Still, they seem to have known him through a consciousness of the reality of the Holy Spirit working in them, bringing their inner life in Christ to maturity. By reason of their baptism they became alive and had access, not merely to a world of precepts and teaching, but to a continuing experience of the risen Christ.

While looking closely at the question of Christian consciousness as it relates to Christian maturity, we can note that a mature Christian life is directed to Christ within. There it assumes a center-to-Center relationship; in other words, an act of love. Love constantly pours energy into the soul bringing with it vitality and new love, generous love. Such a process continues as the soul matures.

This maturing process rouses the psychical man to the level of the spiritual man by drawing on the power of the Holy Spirit within the deepest recesses of the psyche. There, power is released under the gentleness of the Holy Spirit building up our strength in "union with the Lord" (Eph. 6:10). Once we begin to understand the meaning of Christian consciousness, we will realize that the Holy Spirit is not idle within us for he will make us wise and reveal God to us so that we will know him (Eph. 3:15-20).

In the profound region of our human psyche the Holy Spirit diffuses charity as he pours himself out with divine unction in gifts of wisdom, understanding, counsel, knowledge, fortitude, and in gifts of ministry—healing, prophecy, discernment—as needed. He moves over our whole person, becoming the soul of our soul, the life of our life.

Christian maturity is pregnant with meaning and mystery. Just a brief consideration of the subject will call attention to the fact that it is through Christ that we will receive glory (2 Thess. 1:12); it is only he who makes our hearts strong, perfect, and holy (1 Thess. 3:13). Such a thought should discourage those tempted through ignorance or arrogance to pronounce on the spiritual maturity of another or on the state of another's soul.

While Christ dwells in all Christians, he comes alive in us at different times, in different ways, and in different degrees. Christian consciousness has no set rules. But then we ask, What accounts for the difference? Simply the degree of freedom with which we allow the Holy Spirit to work within, a freedom like that given by him to Mary which makes it possible to glorify and praise God on all occasions. We must praise him in suffering as well as success with openness and receptivity, not only in receiving his love, but in allowing it to flow through us—sometimes purifying us, sometimes strengthening us, for ministry. For we need reminding that it is not the amount of suffering, trial, or work in our lives which makes us mature Christians, but how we allow the Holy Spirit to work in us with his healing love.

Saints in Therapy

We are all saints in therapy, and our rate of growth or degree of Christian consciousness is not a matter of self-determination. However, if the activity of the Holy Spirit is experienced, it is bound eventually to show in some way; not necessarily in a remarkable, final, outward transformation of personality, but at least through a change of attitude.

In any case it is the poor in spirit, the spiritually hungry, those who are having a spiritual energy crisis, who are ready to experience Christian consciousness when the Holy Spirit, until then dormant in the depths of the psyche, now comes alive within. Although the naturally endowed may recognize their need for Christ within, because more demands are made on them, the less endowed and the oppressed, through their greater need, also come to this realization. Both arrive at this point not through flawless exegesis or theology but through a love within that comes alive to sustain them. Both are in situations which enable them to mature in differing ways and degrees. Not through pious platitudes or prescriptions, but through his deep, abiding love.

Nice People and New Christians

In an effort to understand Christian consciousness as it relates to a mature life-style I began to realize that there are many Christians today whose psychic structures are deformed and difficult. While they may have had a focal awakening and are struggling with their hangups, their life-style shows every evidence of immaturity. They will never mature as a Francis of Assisi, to charm the birds or caress the wolf of Gubbio. They continually fall, pick themselves up, and keep going—a true test of a maturing Christian. Although they are gradually maturing in the inner being through the strengthening power of the Holy Spirit, their immature traits may often repel others: bad temper, unbalanced personalities, and behavioral patterns generally associated with neurosis. The most that can be said is that they are saints in therapy.

On the other hand, there are Christians endowed with natural goodness, natural gifts, sound nerves, intelligence, good health, and fine upbringing who are regarded generally as nice people and mature Christians. They can ingratiate themselves with others, especially the powers that be, and can always be counted on to do the right thing at the right time. If they don't, few will fuss about it. Some of these are immature moralists who have not really experienced a living awareness of God's love. They are unplugged from the source of spiritual energy, the Holy Spirit, and are running on their own batteries. Given this varied situation it is obvious that the effect of a new Christian consciousness will be quite different on the maturing life-style of these two types.

In reflecting on this situation we can see that natural gifts are good to have and a nasty disposition is to be deplored; every effort should be made to improve it and to prepare the way of the Lord to whatever degree possible. Like the economically rich, however, those with a natural maturity still have spiritual needs, the need for Christ being uppermost. Yet they may be tempted to pride and egocentrism—forms of immaturity. The person with the neurotic disposition, on the other hand, through constant criticism and nonacceptance is tempted to despair. Both have problems. Both may from time to time experience Christian consciousness but not in the same way. The nice person is not necessarily the same as the agnostic who proclaimed to me not so long ago that he had no need of religion, nor of Christ, since he had all he wanted in life. Whether nice or neurotic, it is the person who has a spiritual hunger who will experience the kingdom within; it is a question of "deep calling unto deep." Both nice and nasty persons can stray away, feed on husks for a while, and then suddenly awaken to the treasures in their Father's house.

The most destitute individual with a deformed psychic structure, if revitalized by the Holy Spirit through a "born-again" experience, a focal awakening, a "baptism in the Holy Spirit," tends to become an expression of inner freedom even though this expression may escape outward observation. These are Christians whose maturity is only in germ. They are saints in therapy. In the depths of their spirits they may experience the breathing love of the Holy Spirit which often manifests itself in some unheard-of act of tenderness or generosity.

John Wesley and Francis of Assisi are nearer to the neurotic with a Christian consciousness, whose humility opens him up to a generous though wavering response to the Holy Spirit, than the agnostic with a wholesome psychic structure or the immature moral conformist steeped in material advantages and pride yet devoid of Christian consciousness and genuine love.

If we are considering the relationship between Christian consciousness and maturity, one way to resolve the question is to take a good hard look at scripture. Why not consider Peter after the remarkable experience on Mount Tabor? He seems to be the same blustering man who would hardly do well on a personality profile as Sister Mary Melannie points out, see page 35.

Since growth experiences are as diverse as people, no one save the Holy Spirit actually knows the degree of our maturity. Nonetheless, we ask if there is any way of knowing how spiritually mature we are.

"By their fruits you will know them" has been one familiar way of judging Christians for years. But externals are not precise measurements. We are reminded of Paul's words: "If I give all to the poor, but have not love I am nothing."

Name: Simon Bar-Jonah* **Date:** April 1, 30 A.D. **Comments:**

Trait	1	2	3	4	5	6	7	8	9	10	Trait	Comments
Inactivity Slowness	1	(2)	3	4	5	6	7	8	9	10	General Activity	He tends to act before he thinks.
Impulsiveness	1	2	3	4	5	6	7	8	(9)	10	Restraint	Almost rude at times.
Submissiveness	1	2	3	4	5	6	7	(8)	9	10	Boldness	Frequently tells fish stories.
Dishonesty	1	2	3	(4)	5	6	7	8	9	10	Honesty	Always wants to be no. 1.
Humility	1	2	3	4	5	6	7	(8)	9	10	Pride	
Introversion	1	2	3	4	5	6	7	8	(9)	10	Extroversion	He's apt to betray a friend in a pinch.
Disloyalty	1	2	3	(4)	5	6	7	8	9	10	Loyalty	Easily moved to tears.
Emotional Stability	1	2	3	4	5	6	7	(8)	9	10	Emotional Instability	
Suggestibility	(1)	2	3	4	5	6	7	8	9	10	Independent Thinker	He'd walk on water if someone told him to.
Deprived Environment	1	(2)	3	4	5	6	7	8	9	10	Enriched Environment	Suffers from a culturally deprived childhood.
Tactless	(1)	2	3	4	5	6	7	8	9	10	Tactful	Always putting his foot in his mouth.
Impractical	1	2	(3)	4	5	6	7	8	9	10	Practical	
Good appearance	1	2	3	4	5	6	7	8	(9)	10	Poor appearance	Overweight, heavily bearded, perspires a lot.
Uneducated	1	2	(3)	4	5	6	7	8	9	10	Highly educated	

* Reprinted by permission of the National Catholic Reporter, PO Box 281, Kansas City, Missouri 64141.

The other apostles would hardly have fared much better:

Mr. Jesus Christ
Nazareth
Galilee, Palestine

Dear Mr. Christ:

Several weeks ago you requested that we give our series of psychological tests to the 12 men you were considering as possible associates in your work of ministry.

Although we are still in the process of administering and compiling the results of the tests, we thought you would be anxious to receive the results as soon as possible. Hence, we are enclosing the test results for Mr. Simon Bar-Jonah. His profile sheet accompanies this letter.

As you can tell, Mr. Bar-Jonah's personality is characterized by a dangerous rashness, overt pride, and a lack of emotional stability that would no doubt be detrimental to you and your work. We feel also that his general physical appearance would create a bad image for your proposed organization.

Furthermore, during our research we discovered that Mr. Bar-Jonah is (to put it bluntly) a "lousy" fisherman. We suspect that his lack of success in his current employment is the cause of his willingness to leave all and follow you.

Therefore, based on our testing, we highly recommend that you do *not* consider Mr. Bar-Jonah as a possible associate. We will make further recommendations regarding the fitness of the other 11 as soon as possible. (We've tested all except Mr. Thomas Twin, who failed to show up for his appointment.)

Based on the evidence we have so far, we would recommend only Mr. Judas Iscariot, who has a fine head for financial matters and would no doubt be a real asset to you and your organization.

Sincerely,

Galilee Psychological Testing Service[1]

Spiritual writers say the only way to know something of our maturity is to take a glimpse backward five or ten years. Then we will readily see vast changes in attitudes and a deepening relationship with Christ. One thing we will discover for certain—there is no such thing as "instant and final holiness!" We will learn that the growth process includes an expansion of consciousness, with each new experience like another awakening to life.

A Focal Awakening

As we begin to understand the meaning of maturity in respect to Christian consciousness, we learn that it usually begins with a focal awakening in our growth center, a coming *alive* of the Holy Spirit and of the gifts we received in baptism. In some instances, it is a sudden awakening; in others, a moment of loving communication in a fleeting awareness of God's love and presence, an experience that is sometimes as delicate as the human breath. Describe it as you will; no two people are alike. It is a realization of being loved and of loving a Person at a profound level.

Until this awakening occurs we are much like Teresa of Avila who wrote that even though she was aware that she had a soul, she neither appreciated its worth nor remembered the One who lived in it, because she had allowed her eyes to be blinded by the vain things of this life.

As we mature in our focal faith there are heavy shadows, idols, and bondages to deal with. We are still earthbound. Somehow, we do not fully realize the worth of this new dimension of faith consciousness, nor do we yet have that liberty which marks a more intimate communion. At this time, it is not so much a matter of sin which holds us back, as our "holy" idols, our "sacred" phobias, which offer a barrier to the inflow of God's love.

In other words, our personal hangups get in the way of a pure relational faith of loving communication with God.

Thomas Merton, in a circular letter written to some of his friends, mentioned a monk who gave up great worldly prosperity, but upon entering the monastery got hung up on a pet cow, which for him became somewhat of a golden calf. The first commandment, "Thou shalt not have strange gods before me," needs careful watching at all stages of the maturing process. For as Merton says, our sacred cows can impede the maturing process and get us off-focus for an occasional fall.

Christian Reality and Appearance

John Mackay notes that Christians by and large tend to focus on religious appearances rather than reality.[2] They tend to make the means the end. According to Mackay, we become so absorbed in ideas about God, about the Bible, and about Jesus Christ, that little emphasis is placed on Jesus Christ as a personal, indwelling presence. We are committed to systems of thought, our favorite Bible quotations, our committee meetings, our liturgical refinements, rather than to a maturing inward relationship with Christ himself. Our focus becomes blurred. We theologize, moralize, legalize, but fail to realize this loving presence of Christ in us as the core reality in our lives. Yet his presence is the essence of our focal faith as it develops into an inward relational love.

What is important to note in Mackay's observations that the same tendency to get off-focus, by overintellectualizing, oversystematizing, and overorganizing, is now evident in the heavy focus on fringe aspects of Christian consciousness popularized in endless testifying. Some Christians who have had a focal awakening, but are not yet established in an inward-faith relationship, come on strong as they recount a break-through experience with no mention of Christ's love and presence. It reminds me of the cock in *The Creature's Choir* by Carmen Bernos de Gasztold. He pleads that the Lord not forget about him, for even though he is indeed a humble servant, it is he who in fact makes the sun rise; the

Lord should understand that while he is his humble servant, he does need some glitter and ostentation.

I recently heard a Presbyterian pastor give a remarkable discourse on the intimate communion relationship with God found in John's Gospel. When the pastor finished his talk, the young choir director rushed to the podium and announced: "I just want you all to know that today is the anniversary of when I first spoke in tongues." Paul's letter to the immature Corinthians needs to be taken very seriously, even literally, these days. He warned some of the Corinthians that they were making an idol of what was simply a refreshing and invigorating way of praising God.

The danger, however, of these gifts taking the place of the Giver of Gifts, can indeed be very real. It reminds me of what Rabindranath Tagore wrote in *None But God's Presence:*

> Time after time I came to your gate with raised hands, asking for more and yet more. You gave and gave, now in slow measure, now in sudden excess. . . . Take, oh take—has now become my cry. . . . hold my hands, raise me from the still-gathering heap of your gifts into the bare infinity of your uncrowded presence.[3]

This raises the question of whether becoming too engrossed in our own spiritual maturing process could in itself become a holy hangup. Wouldn't this be just another form of egocentrism, or immaturity? My answer: Such insight often has merit for both our inspiration and encouragement. And at the same time, it provides us with opportunities to praise God for all he has done for us and in us. Then, like Mary, we can burst into song: "My soul magnifies the Lord and my spirit rejoices in God my Savior . . . for he has done great things to me and holy is his name" (Luke 1:46-49).

Focal Faith— The Beginning of Christian Consciousness

As our idols diminish through our response to the powerful love of the Holy Spirit, this focal relationship develops into a loving communication. The doors of perception are opened up more fully as all life takes on new meaning. Now, a real sense of our existence is revealed in this brilliant focus, a Reality of the highest order.

Christian consciousness is the experience of those numerous Christ-in-you passages of Scripture that relate to Christian mystery and the plan of the redemption. In its focal awakening stage it is a growing communication with God. In the context of prayer and meditation it means, "We rest in him as he works in us." In the context of action it means, "A *ruling* sense of God's presence." In the highest range of consciousness it is communion with God. Christian consciousness is not unusual for it is simply a coming alive of the Holy Spirit deep within our inmost psyche. Jungian psychology claims that the floor of the unconscious is the religious unconscious. And when the religious unconscious reaches the level of consciousness this is the equivalent of what Scripture is referring to as the kingdom of God within!

An important insight here is that Christian consciousness, as it relates to the maturing process, is not something to be desired of itself. It pertains rather to our desire to see the work of Christ made real in us and through us. It goes without saying that if we experience a growing relationship with him, we are bound to feel different, and in our ministry to others our natural talents will be enhanced by the love, power, and vitality of the Holy Spirit. The end or aim of maturity is God's glory; and it is in a mature, abiding relationship, at times more conscious than others, that we give God glory and bear fruit in abundance (John 15:8).

To the degree we abide in him . . . will we mature . . . will we bear fruit. It is is important, however, to realize that while we may begin to experience a maturing Christian consciousness in this life, its effects will not be complete in this life, because death is an important part of the treatment. Until then, how we mature is indeed a mystery known to God alone, for we are all "saints in therapy."

Christian consciousness is an awareness of a deep relational love-faith which is essentialy a life of communion with God. This "vertical" communion with God has as its consequence a "horizontal" relationship of communion with fellow Christians. It includes the experience of the continual deepening of this relational love-faith from communication to communion as part of the Christian growth process, as well as growth in an activated faith centered in Christ's love, with power to live and to give expressed in a life of *prayer in action.*

Christian Maturity as:

Growth in Relational Faith

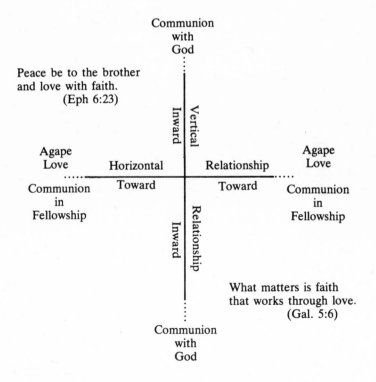

Chapter III
Probing Our Roots

An experience of Christian consciousness is far richer than that relationship with God enjoyed in Old Testament times. It also lacks the extravagances feared by some conservative Christians of "absorption in the Deity." This priceless gift was given to us by Jesus and was made available for all people through his death and resurrection, followed by the gift of the Holy Spirit. Paul does everything in his power to express this experience in words. He also makes it clear that we do not deserve the glory of this intimacy, a relationship lost by Adam and regained by Jesus, which we now experience.

For, as we realize, it is only through Christ that we come into communion with God, the source of our love of others, in a deep relational faith experience. As we mature, we begin to realize more and more that Christ is in us and we in him and that in some mysterious way we will be with him in glory, as we begin to experience him now, on the way to glory.

There is a scriptural passage that helps us understand how Christian consciousness relates to the Trinity. Jesus indicated at the Last Supper that not only would he return to his own friends, but the Father would come also, Jesus and the Father would come together. "We will make our home with you" (John 14:23). And this includes the Holy Spirit whom Jesus had already promised as a lasting presence in our hearts (John 14:16-17). The indwelling presence is that of the blessed Trinity.

Thomas Merton claims that communion with God, the highest consciousness, as it relates to a new life in the kingdom, was generally left in the background by the liberal Christianity of the nineteenth and early twentieth centuries. But anyone who reads the New Testament objectively must admit that this is the doctrine of the first Christians without which Christianity is only a moral system with little spiritual consistency.[1] There is a need today to return to our roots.

The Heart of the Christian Faith

Communion with God, the highest expression of Christian consciousness, is closely related with Christian maturity and is linked with every aspect of Christianity. It may in fact be called the heart of the Christian faith. There is much put in other terms, often confusing, which might well be put in terms of communion. For the goal of the mature Christian life is essentially a life of communion with God. The maturing process in terms of consciousness involves an awareness of God's presence (experienced sometimes as absence) which grows from loving communication to intimate communion. It is an ever-deepening relationship with God and an agape relationship with others, leading to an activated faith which embraces the world.

We find frequent references in the writings of Paul and John to this conscious awareness of Christ within. The New Testament as a whole gives us a picture of rich intimate communion with God which is not the special privilege of a few but actually the everyday life of the normal Christian.

Paul seemed especially impatient to share this fact about the Christian life. He spoke of it frequently and in many contexts. But why did he call it a secret? Was it because he felt that like Christians today some of his hearers might be too immature to understand or to realize that this great blessing was meant for all? Paul speaks of God's plan as "this rich and glorious secret which he has for all peoples. And the secret is that Christ is in you, which means you will share the glory of God" (Col. 1:27 GNB).

Paul strains himself to make sure that growing Christians are sure to grasp this mystery, that the indwelling presence of Christ is understood as the very essence of the mature Christian life. "Do you understand," he says, "that you are God's temple and that God's Spirit has his dwelling in you? It is a holy thing, this temple of God which is nothing other than yourselves" (I Cor. 3:16-17). For the benefit of the immature Corinthians (we are all beginners at one stage of growth or another), Paul repeats himself: "Surely you know that your bodies are the shrines of the Holy Spirit, who dwells in you." Then he observes that this is a grace that on the basis of good behavior they really don't deserve. "He is God's gift to you for which a great price was paid." How then should we respond? He tells us to glorify God by making our bodies shrines for his presence (I Cor. 6:19-20).

While I was reflecting on all of this and reading the writings of John the Evangelist, Paul's words began to take on new meaning. John has much to say about Christian consciousness as he completes the revelations of Paul. He uses the word *mansio*, meaning "abode," derived from the verb *meno*, "to dwell," forty times in his Gospel and twenty-three times in his First Epistle. Why is this so significant? Simply because "abode" is a word which implies intimacy and stability. As we mature in relation to our Christ-consciousness it is no longer a matter of one dramatic awakening, but rather of Christ becoming an abiding presence.

How Does Christian Consciousness Differ?

Christian consciousness differs from other forms of religious consciousness simply because it is related to the Christian mystery of Christmas, Easter, and Pentecost. It is the realization of these mysteries in our psyche in different ways and at different times. It is experiencing the incarnation as expressed by John the Evangelist, "The word became flesh and dwelt among us" (John 1:14); or by Paul, "It is no longer I who live, but Christ who lives in me," or "I rejoice in my weakness because the power of Christ becomes manifest." It is the mystery of death and resurrection on the experiential level, a gradual dying and coming to new life, an experience of "metanoia," a change of heart as we begin to share the grace of Christ's triumph through the power of the Holy Spirit in our inmost psyche. We often think of the mysteries of Christ's life in a historic sense or in relation to liturgical worship and the sacraments as we commemorate the great celebrations of Christmas, Easter, and Pentecost. But we are less likely to identify these mysteries as coming alive in our own personal lives. Yet this is what Christian consciousness is all about.

Thomas Merton refers to Christian consciousness in relation to Christian mystery as a deep peace and a simple openness to God at every moment. He says that when we speak of experiencing the mysteries of Christ, we simply mean a realization in the very depths of our being that God has chosen us and loved us from all eternity, that we are really his children, and we are really loved by him; that there is really a personal bond between us, and he is really present. It is so simple Merton claims that there is no need to make a fuss about it.[2]

These comments remind me of something a mother told me regarding her son of three who had startled her by sharing an intimate secret: "God is in me," he whispered, "and God is love!" The consciousness of "Christ in me" is not a matter of chronological age. This reality may come alive in any Christian. I recall an ineffable awareness of his love and presence within as I was visiting the Church of Notre Dame in Paris. I felt like a little church within a church. This great Cathedral of Notre Dame in which God dwelt was symbolic of another living temple in which Jesus took up his abode as the Holy Spirit rested on Mary.

My friend the late Dr. Albert E. Day, Methodist pastor and founder of the "Disciplined Order of Christ," recorded these inspiring insights in *The Captivating Presence* shortly before his death: "My own experience, I think has something to say here, just because I am such an ordinary person who faced the ordinary lot of man with such ordinary gifts." He then describes his consciousness of dying and becoming alive in Christ as he lay on a hospital bed. In the depths of human anguish, he wrote that he was not asking God that his pain be less, that he be exempted from the common lot, or that he be saved from the fate of others whose bodies were also torturing them. But he said he was asking for the consciousness of "His Presence." "O my God," he wrote, "I cry by day but thou dost not answer; by night but I find no rest. My soul thirsts for the living God . . ." He continues:

> Then all at once I was made aware of the Presence. I did not *see* any image . . . nor was there any sort of phantom appearing and disappearing. Nor did I hear a voice. But within that darkness, I became *certain of a presence*. It gave birth to a *new consciousness* within me, opened me up to a new world of truth, beauty, love and beckoned me to enter and make it my *home* forever. It was the Spirit so captivating that my spirit responded with eager gladness (italics added).

He then insists that if one does not have this consciousness, all other things are inadequate to give life meaning and glory. He claims that there is nothing to equal the ministry of the Presence in its power to keep us aware of the total reality of our daily lives and to keep us on the path of heroic devotion and decisive action in every area of life.[3] This is what prayer in action is all about.

Christian vs. Oriental Consciousness

Christianity has not been behind other religions in its understanding of altered states of consciousness and forms of prayer and meditation which "prepare the way of the Lord" and allow an easier access into the spiritual realm; that is, those forms of prayer and contemplation similar to Yoga and Zen. However, we need to be mindful of very fundamental differences. In Yoga, the concentration of human powers is in itself a goal. Whereas in Christian consciousness the goal is Christ within, a goal which always ensures a positive not a neutral or negative result.

As we look at expanded consciousness in Buddhism we find it is based on the life of humanity before Adam's fall and assumes a humanity in no need of salvation, whereas Christian consciousness is a transforming experience, a new creation (Eph. 1:7-10; 4:23-24) effected through the death and resurrection of Christ. This new life in Christ so far surpasses the life of Adam before the fall that it evoked those famous words from Augustine, "Happy fault which merited so great a Redeemer!"

In making a distinction between Christian consciousness and Zen, Merton notes that the fulfillment of Zen is love. Unlike Christianity, however, Zen seems to lack a transcendent *personal* center on which love can converge. And this Center, he points out, is the "Risen and Deathless Christ" in whom all are fulfilled in one. This personal centering in Christ not only distinguishes Christianity from Zen but also from Marxism and from popular psychic and "selfist" meditation.

Christian Consciousness and Selfism

Some pseudo-psychic religious awareness groups today woo their Christian clients with the point that their techniques are adaptable to any form of religious consciousness. In theory this sounds good. But the problem as I see it is that their many Christian clients, intrigued by the glib use of Christian terminology, are thoroughly unfamiliar with the essence of Christian consciousness. How then can they integrate their experiences, particularly if they are immature and intrigued with psychic phenomena—which may have religious overtones, such as visions, voices, and the like, but in terms of Christian consciousness as understood here, are at best immature experiences.

Christian consciousness is not and cannot be rooted in selfist psychology. For as we move out from our limited self we enter a new kind of existence and discover an inner motivating love which enables us to see everything in relation to it. Mature Christian experience is not ego-oriented, but rather Christ-oriented. As indicated above, it does not grow from concentrating on: "How great I am," but on "How great Thou art!" It is a renouncing of our hangups as we experience a new freedom *in* Christ. It is an experience of human nature gradually being changed as we renounce ourselves and become centered in that deepest of realities—the highest consciousness—communion with God. In its beginning stages it is a new awareness and actualization of ourselves in relation to him. We are redeemed by him, transformed by him, and glorified in and with him.

Our Spiritual Roots

There is much inspiration in the writings of the early Christians and the fathers of the church on the subject of the indwelling presence of God. The early Christians looked upon themselves as *Godbearers*. Eusebius tells us how Leonidas, the father of Origen, used to kneel down and kiss his sleeping child inhabited by the Holy Spirit.

In general, a familiarity with our Christian roots will show that the early Christians *experienced* Christ before they wrote about him. The theology and reflection of the New Testament and the early church was based upon a living encounter with Jesus and his Father and the continued experience of Jesus through the Holy Spirit sent at Pentecost. Christian theology flows in part from an experience of Christ. The early fathers held that what the soul is to the body, the Holy Spirit is to the soul, its life principle.

Ignatius of Antioch, martyr and apostle of the indwelling presence, coined both for himself and for every Christian the surname *theophoros,* or the "bearer of God." "All of you," he wrote to the Ephesians, "are bearers of God . . . bearers of

Christ." The temple of Jerusalem, made by man's hand, has yielded to the living temple, "the sanctuary of the Body of Christ, the center of worship in spirit and truth." Thus every Christian who has Christ in his heart through faith (Eph. 3:17) is in turn a temple of the living God.

St. Augustine looked everywhere for God and ended up finding him in his own heart. "Return to your heart and find him. . . . O Beauty ever ancient, ever new, too late have I known thee, too late have I loved thee. And behold thou wast within me whilst I was without seeking thee. . . . Thou wast with me . . . but I was not with thee." Augustine wrote in one of his sermons that God's dwelling within you is more real than if he were in front of your very eyes outside you. If you receive Christ in your room he is with you, but is he not with you when you receive him into your heart?[4]

The fact that the soul is truly a heaven in which God dwells is applied by several great spiritual writers to the Lord's Prayer. "Our Father who art in heaven" is interpreted as meaning the "heaven of our soul." Teresa of Avila, much like Augustine, regretted how she neglected the great King dwelling in the little palace of her soul.

In this era of expanded consciousness, the more we probe our spiritual roots the more we will begin to realize that the highest consciousness is to be found in that rich and glorious secret, "Christ in you." And as we mature in our own awareness of him, we will understand more fully those words of Paul, "I ask God . . . that Christ will make his home in your hearts . . . and that you will have your roots and foundation in love" (Eph. 3:17).

The Indwelling Presence and the Eucharist

Consciousness of the indwelling presence of God complements his presence in the Eucharist. While this is meaningful to Catholics, Methodists, Episcopalians, and Lutherans, in particular, it is likewise becoming increasingly meaningful to some evangelicals who, while enjoying the consciousness of Christ within, have until recently kept wholly apart from the sacramental aspects of Christianity. On the other hand, those Christians for whom an experience of the sacramental Christ has been focal, may in the future need to give more attention to the real presence of Christ within them.

The two indwellings are complementary. Jesus gave the revelation concerning the Eucharist and then that of his indwelling presence. After the Eucharistic Communion was established he revealed in his final words of farewell in the upper room that we could anticipate an intimate relationship, an intimacy of eternal life, both through the Eucharist and his indwelling presence. (In the Roman Catholic understanding, a deep inner life prepares us for the Eucharist, while the healing power of the Eucharist enriches our inner life. Little mention will be made of the Eucharist, not because it is of little importance to the writer, but simply because it is not within the scope of this book.)

The Maturing Process: Natural and Spiritual

Our inner life matures in wavy lengths. There are constant ups and downs. There are times when we find ourselves empty and hollow. These are the times when we should not force ourselves to meditate. There are laws in the spiritual growth process that are reflected in the laws of nature as well as in Christian mystery—the death to life process, for instance. Brother Lawrence was struck by this natural process on seeing a tree stripped of its leaves in the winter when he considered that within a little time the leaves would be renewed, and after that the flowers and fruit would appear. He received a revelation of the providence and power of God which never left his soul. This experience freed him from the world and awakened in him such a great love for God that he could not tell whether it had increased forty years later.[5]

As we develop mature prayer habits and a supportive

life-style, God usually allows us to take the first steps toward him. At times we think we are really on top of things and are maturing according to our own outlay of effort. Of course, this is a great boost for our ego. Self-confidence mounts as we begin to feel calm and secure as a result of a well-regulated and clearly monitored spiritual life in our growth center. No ego-oriented meditation fads are needed at this point to bolster our spiritual smugness—a peculiarity of the beginning stages of the spiritual growth process.

Once we have had a focal awakening, however, the maturing process develops inwardly into a relational faith and an inward loving communication with God. Christ then begins to detach us from our superstitous ways. He turns our once well-ordered growth center upside down and makes us understand that the essential matter is not our activity so much as our docility to his guidance.

Gradually, the Holy Spirit ministers to us as we learn the secret of true dependence on him. Then as we become docile to his grace, God's power begins to work more fully in us and through us.

To sum up, there are not only similarities between the spiritual maturing process and the natural growth process, there are likewise contrasts, contrasts which upset achievers. However, as the process becomes better understood through the inspiration of the Holy Spirit, the meaning of maturity as it relates to Christian consciousness will take on new meaning. However, when we compare the natural and spiritual aspects of the growth process, there are certain aspects of it which are difficult for us to understand in our achievement-oriented culture; simply because these are the reverse of the natural process. For instance, when we begin to grow out of adolescence into adulthood, normally speaking, we begin to assume more initiative, responsibility, and the fruitful use of our abilities and talents. On the other hand, in the area of Christian consciousness, as we mature we develop a receptivity to the Holy Spirit and a docility to his whisperings and inspiration. We allow our natural abilities to be enhanced and enriched as the gifts of ministry develop in our lives. Of course, the ideal of Christian maturity is a blending of the two aspects of our maturing lives, the natural and the spiritual. Once again, when and how we develop is unique in the lives of each one of us.

MATURITY:

NATURAL	SPIRITUAL
initiative	listening
activity	receptivity
responsibility	docility
use of natural talents	natural talents enriched by the power of the Holy Spirit and gifts of ministry

THE IDEAL: A BLEND OF THE TWO

In general, the question which often comes up in regard to Christian consciousness and maturity brings up again the question of Christian mystery. Isn't Christianity a way of the cross—why all this euphoria? Some Christians introduced into this way of life seem to be on an all-time high. On the other hand, the Holy Spirit has yet to be activated in the lives of some who have been good servants of God for years, going along on an even keel. There are many ways of looking at this question. Some relate to differences in personality and background. Others pertain to characteristics of the spiritual growth process on the level of expanded consciousness. These characteristics are directly related to Christian mystery. We can gain insight on the matter by comparing the viewpoints of the two Christian traditions: the Eastern and Western traditions.

Eastern Orthodox Christians say that the Apostles were admitted to the joy of the Resurrection without having first experienced the Cross. In fact, they insist, they ran from it. Later, however, they knew the meaning of the cross through their own martyrdom, for which they had been strengthened by the glory of their earlier experience.

Western Christians favor gradual growth through the Cross to a fuller life in Christ, which transforms them into his very likeness, in ever greater degrees of glory (II Cor. 3:18).

In this regard, a monk of the Eastern Orthodox Church would observe that the sinner cannot experience the cross if he or she had not first received the strength of the risen Christ. Rising with Christ remains the necessary condition for dying with him. Rising will always be out of reach if the presence of the risen Lord and the victorious grace of his resurrection is not imparted as a free gift, prior to any sacrificial decision on our part. There is a difference in approach between East and West. Both acknowledge the correlation of Good Friday and Easter Sunday, but the respective order of these two mysteries is seen differently.[6]

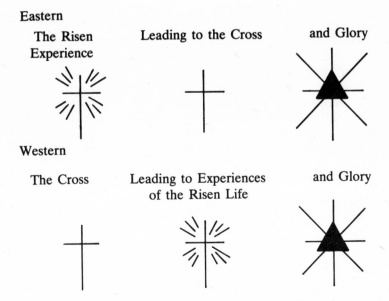

Eastern

The Risen Experience   Leading to the Cross   and Glory

Western

The Cross   Leading to Experiences of the Risen Life   and Glory

Chapter IV

From Communication to Communion with God

Growing Pangs and Pains

To grow in a relational love-faith with Christ in you is what Christianity is all about. You can readily see that maturity, presence, and union with Christ are all closely linked together in Paul's preaching. "So we preach Christ to everyone. . . . in order to bring each one into God's presence as a *mature* individual in *union* with Christ" (Col. 1:28 RSV, italics added).

As you grow in maturity, the Holy Spirit spiritualizes your soul and transforms you. Paul does not say you will be transformed, but that you are being transformed (II Cor. 3:18). It is a gradual and continuous process from communication to communion. After a focal awakening and the beginning of a new love-communication with Christ within, there are intermittent experiences of intimate communion. It is something like moving back and forth on a four-lane highway until you finally get settled in one lane and continue on toward your destination. Thomas Merton once said that there is not just one awakening, but many break-through experiences, each followed by a plateau until the next breakthrough. Gregory of Nyssa, an Eastern father of the church, insists that we never stop growing and that we should never place a limit on maturity or perfection.

In the beginning, while you are still learning to use your former idols as so much fuel for the flame of love, your moorings in this new mode of religious awareness are not all that deep. You are in an in-between state. There is a sense of loss for the day that has gone, and a longing for the day that is yet to come. It is a time when the loving communication in your growth center has not yet matured to an intimate communion. It is a time when your spirit is keenly aware of its lack of love, a condition that John of the Cross refers to as love-sickness.

> Love-sickness has no other remedy than the presence of the Beloved. The reason for this is that love of God is the soul's health and the soul does not have full health until love is complete. When the soul has not a single degree of love, it is dead. When love is perfect she will have full health.[1]

What you may not realize, as your inward relational faith is deepening, is that your very concern about not loving is in effect a form of loving. In your former do-it-yourself "how great I am" stage when your Christian life was partly conscience with no Christ-consciousness, such a thing never bothered you. John of the Cross insists that when you have this love-sickness, the painful feeling of lacking love merely shows that you have some love, because you are aware of what you lack by comparison with what you have. If you do not experience love-sickness, he claims there are two possible explanations: (a) you have no love at all, or (b) you are perfect in love.

A third explanation might be added in light of numerous Christians today whose love-life in Christ has been activated through prayer ministry, contemplation, or the Eucharist. Since the beginning of life, love has been in them but, as Paul says, it has not been stirred up. It has been nesting in their growth center as a latent love waiting to be activated.

Bear in mind, that even though the activity of the Holy Spirit has not yet reached a level of consciousness, he is not idle in our growth center. He is there helping us to develop a focal faith, to center us on the center of reality. As we gradually recognize our idols as appearances and turn them over to him, he is there cleansing, healing, and unifying us as he weans us from them.

Merton says that if we really want to mature we must let God build us into one piece. This is something he alone can do by bringing us to new levels of awareness. In the awakened soul spiritual growing pains are very real. During this period when we may feel inclined to engage in simple prayer forms which nurture the life of the Spirit within and do not distract us from the central brilliant focus of his loving presence. This form of contemplation is expressed in the phrase "rest in him as he works in you."

John of the Cross explains in *Dark Night of the Soul* and elsewhere that no matter how hard we work at it we cannot purify ourselves for an intimate communion with Christ unless he himself takes us in hand. He describes the process in terms of fire and flame. Following a focal awakening, as already noted, there are periods of gnawing, arid absence described as love-sickness. This is the experience of the Holy Spirit entering deep within our psyche as the soul's disorders are brought forth, disgorged, and healed by the Spirit of God.[2] We may feel like our heart is being placed on the coals as mentioned in Tobias 6:8.

We are now at a period of the maturing process when the poisons in our growth center—pride, vanity, laziness—are being dealt with through the love power of the Holy Spirit in the depth of our center in the realms of the unconscious. There, through loving contemplation, not only is the guilt of special sins removed, but those evil inclinations which have been irritated by sin are healed.

The author of the *Mysticism of the Cloud of Unknowing* calls this maturing process in your growth center the blind stirring of love. He writes convincingly that fasting, sorrow for sin, and tears over the sufferings of Christ, although good in themselves, cannot reach that part of the human psyche which can only be purified and beautified by the "blind stirring of love." This love not only destroys the roots of sin to the degree possible in this life but also begets virtue.[3]

How We Grow

In other words, this inward relational faith transforms our hearts through the love power of the Holy Spirit and brings us to a freedom from sin akin to that which we will enjoy in glory. Ranguin points out that the intimacy of wordless prayer in the depths of the human psyche can do more through the love power of the Holy Spirit to heal our psyches than psychoanalysis. He claims that while we can personally fight against evil tendencies by our own efforts combined with the assistance of grace, we can do practically nothing against those powers buried in the deepest recesses of our souls. We cannot of ourselves descend that far into ourselves and on our own come to grips with those mysterious forces which are the sources of our activity. He writes that

> Even psychoanalysis must remain incomplete because it cannot go deep enough to reach the point where I am placed by God in his presence as His image, capable of entering into dialogue with Him, and where at the same time, I remain so much myself that my normal tendency is to close myself up against God by asserting my personality.[4]

Growth Hazards

As we grow in the use of wordless prayer, deeper forms of meditation, and the practice of the presence of God, we will discover a new harmony and wholeness beginning to develop. It is prayer in this range of consciousness that must be used to nurture our spiritual life as we grow from communication to communion. While our fears should be taken into consideration, they should not be allowed to impede our progress; we should learn to deal with them.

Dr. Elmer Green, a leading neurologist, warns that too hasty a descent into the unconscious indeed offers hazards. Since most humans are not free from personality dross, all kinds of fear and conflict can surface when we relax in contemplative prayer. Theologian William Johnston speaks about this in *Silent Music*. First, he says, we enter into a deeper level of awareness under the guidance of the Holy Spirit, and as this happens certain things occur in our psyche. (a) The mind is expanded, (b) the unconscious is opened up, (c) the memory is stimulated and the past becomes luminous, and (d) joy and sadness, love and hate often surge up. However, we should be prepared for all this. And what should be our reaction?

We should let it be. In fact, we should not resist experiencing our fears, yet we should refuse to analyse what is going on. Why? Because there is something more important to engage our attention, and that is the love which will flow from the depths of our growth center. The evil one is powerless to violate the inner core of our being. While activity is going on in our imaginative and sensory faculties at the outer circle of consciousness, we are imbibing deep wisdom and love in the inner circle of our growth center.

Not only that, but the wounds of the past are exposed to the healing power of the Holy Spirit and are beautifully transfigured "because God's love has been poured into our hearts through the Holy Spirit which has been given to us" (Rom. 5:5). With respect to this George Maloney writes:

Today God has revealed much about the workings of the human psyche through the discoveries made in depth-psychology and psychotherapy. If we are to attain an integrated personality, to harmonize all the various levels of psychic life within our minds, the upper layers of the psyche must be harmonized with the lower layers. This means that the lower layers must be opened up to the scrutiny of the consciousness. Man will always remain crippled and a victim of primordial factors in his life unless he opens up these lower layers. The Christian opens up the dark areas of his unconscious in order that the healing power of God's love revealed by the Word of God, can filter into that broken demonic world and bring it into a loving harmony and wholeness.[5]

The great masters of spiritual life, such as Teresa of Avila, make clear that the fear involved in wordless prayer and contemplation as you grow from loving communication to intimate communion with "Christ in you" should not keep you from venturing into the unknown. For if you are to mature beyond pure external morality and conventional religion, you must face your fears head on. To ignore the healing and purifying effects of the work of the Holy Spirit as your inner life is being nurtured through contemplation and the practice of the presence of God, is to settle for a life of immaturity; a life on the surface; a life of a performer, an achiever. Actually, the hazards for one with a focal faith are not all that great.

Catherine of Siena says that the coming of love is the first real breakthrough in the spiritual life. Self-love holds us bound. We have to risk letting the subconscious play its part. If we let go, we will find that the seed of the kingdom of God has already been sown there, and that the Holy Spirit is already at work. We will then arrive at an equilibrium within, centered not on the dross-filled self, but on Jesus Christ himself.

This, of course, brings up a concern which you may have been thinking about and that is the hazards involved in fad-meditation where the focus is on "How great I am," rather than, "How great Thou art!" If we descend into the deeper levels of consciousness while concentrating on a tarnished ego, we let ourselves loose in a strange vacuum rather than being centered on a personal Christ within. Self-oriented approaches only bring out in bold relief the authenticity of Christian meditation and the necessity of yielding to the guidance and love of the Holy Spirit within.

As you become docile to the Holy One who is alive in your growth center as your Minister par excellence, the hazards of the earlier stages of the maturing process will gradually cease, and your ego-dross will be cleared away. This is not just a pious hope.

This is what Christians through the centuries have both experienced and taught. This is what many today, who are experiencing an outpouring of the Holy Spirit in their growth center, tell us. It is indeed important that we understand this aspect of our maturing process so that we will be encouraged to continue in our desire to grow from loving communication to intimate communion and be more devoted in the practice of the presence of God.

From Communication to Communion

As time goes on, the activity in our growth center seems to change, but it is really we who are changed. The same flame of love, the Holy Spirit, is there, but we are different. As we mature we are cleansed, healed, and unified. The "Living Flame" is no longer oppressive but gentle as we abide in intimate communion with Christ. John of the Cross writes:

Hence the very flame that is now gentle, since it has entered within the soul, is that which was formerly oppressive, assailing it from without.

Now you are not oppressive . . . not dark as you were before, but You are the divine light of my intellect . . . You are the strength of my will, no longer heavy . . . to my soul but rather its glory and delight. . . .[6]

In an era which until recently placed reason supreme over love, a vast number of Christians have understood God's intimate presence intellectually, rather than experientially. You were told that the miraculous New Testament experiences were a matter of history—not for now. Yet with increasing numbers in all denominations coming into an awareness of the Holy Spirit of God's love and presence, you can be assured that the new level of consciousness, particularly of the kind experienced by the Apostles between Easter and Pentecost— root Christianity—is meant likewise for us.

Scripture says: "When that day comes, you will learn for yourselves that I am in my Father, and you are in me and I am in you" (John 14:20). The Semitic term used here for "day," *yom*, indicates a period of time, a word the prophets often used when referring to great interventions of the Lord God. Here

Jesus refers to the time between Easter and Pentecost, a time of extraordinary personal graces which ushered in a new *era* of religious consciousness. Through a very gentle and sure experiential knowledge, we too, will learn for ourselves. The fathers of the church and all the great masters of the spiritual life made it clear that the maturing process is never-ending. With some it never reaches a level of awareness in this life by reason of a stupor of finite and fallen consciousness. With others, as already noted, the maturing process is experienced for long periods as absence rather than presence. But the process will continue for all on into eternity. No one Christian can have the arrogance to claim greater maturity than another Christian, for while there are certain factors common to the spiritual growth process, each Christian is unique in how he or she develops. Moreover, a maturing Christian is not one who doesn't fall; rather one who gets up and keeps growing.

The Mystery of Maturity

In the context of Christian mystery the growth process should be understood for what it really is—a death to life experience. In the awakened soul, spiritual growing pains are real. Christian consciousness opens the door of the psyche to an invasion of another order which transforms the quality of our existence. "Not only creation, but we ourselves, who have the first fruits of the Spirit, groan inwardly as we wait for adoption as sons" (Rom. 8:23). As changes take place gradually within the inner core of our being, there is a transfer of focus from self to God—from death to life. That distance which once separated us from intimate communion with God in paradise is gradually overcome through the purifying, healing, and unifying love of the Holy Spirit within our growth center. A state of peace, delight, and gentleness of love begins in us.

Then, in a communion of love, we begin to experience God's breath, that paradise of intimate relationship with God who created us out of pure love, as recounted in Genesis. Generally speaking, as our spiritual life deepens, the maturing process seems different. The pangs and pains lessen, we begin to think that the activity of the Holy Spirit has changed, but really, it is we who have changed. Christianity is more than a belief; it is an experience. The early Christians saw communion with God as a solid reality, more filled with being and certitude than any other experience of the physical world. In this sense, they were more realistic.

According to the masters of Eastern Christian spirituality, communion with God is not something extraordinary, but is the ordinary development of the Christian called to maturity at the time of baptism and Eucharistic Communion, as inspiringly expressed in

> The Father, the Son, and the Holy Spirit are calling you. . . . They are ready to come down towards you and in you, in order to live as the habitual guests of your soul. They promise to your whole being, . . . a transformation . . . resplendent and glorious.[7]

Communion: A Fruitful Relationship

"Whoever abides in me, and I in him, will bear much fruit" (John 15:5). The mature Christian's life, light, spiritual strength, and capacity to love God in deep communion and his fellowman in agape love come to him from a divinity within yet are manifest without in his own life and the world of human experience. The words of John summarize not only the incarnation but the heart of the growth experience: "And the Word became flesh and dwelt among us, full of grace and truth; we have beheld his glory, glory as of the only Son from the Father. . . . And from his fullness have we all received, grace upon grace" (John 1:14, 16).

Maturing in Christ as we grow in our relationship from communication to communion is our goal in life. So often, as has been noted, Christians have viewed growth in terms of performance while overlooking that inner quality of being which begins with a brilliant focus and gradually develops into intimate communion with the indwelling Holy Spirit. As the Holy Spirit reproduces Christ in us, the fruits of his incarnational presence become visible. Just as the Holy Spirit was the origin and principle of Christ's incarnation in Mary, his activity in each Christian is as real as the historical Incarnation. The Incarnation reaches its goal by spiritualizing us and forming us in the character of Christ. It is only when such a profound mystery fails to seep into deep consciousness that immature Christians feed on the husks of popularized forms of reincarnation.

Writers throughout the centuries have attempted to describe this incarnational presence and its fruitfulness in the life of the Christian in terms of transformation in Christ. One such effort was made by Simone Weil.

> The Holy Spirit is . . . the seed which falls on every soul. To receive it, the soul must become . . . a vessel; something . . . passive like water. Then the seed becomes an embryo, and at last a child; Christ is born in the soul. What used to be called "I" and "me" is destroyed . . . and in place of it there is a new being, grown from seed that fell from God into the soul. That is what it is to be born anew; to be born of water and the spirit; to be born of God and not of the will of man. . . . After this operation, "I no longer live, but Christ lives in me." . . . Our soul ought to be nothing except a place of welcome and nourishment for this divine germ.[8]

No matter how limited human efforts are to describe communion with God and its effects, what needs to be borne in mind is that it is a fruitful relationship. As we are united with Christ in loving awareness and communion, the fruit gives glory to the Father, for separated from him we can do nothing (John 15:5). Evidence of the qualities of Christ will begin to appear in us: "Your lives will be filled with the true qualities which Jesus Christ alone can produce, for the glory and praise of God" (Phil. 1:11).

Love, joy, peace, kindness, goodness, faithfulness, gentleness, self-control; these qualities mentioned in Galatians 5:22-23 are the fruit of the Spirit. These are the product of his incarnational presence bearing fruit in the depths of our growth center as we commune there with him. And the more we mature in communion with him there, the more fruitful will we become and the more glory will we give to God: "Then everyone will glorify God because of the results they see in you" (2 Thess. 1:12).

The mysterious phrase "my soul magnifies the Lord" has many implications and applications for us. For as we grow in communion with God, the fruits of the Holy Spirit mature in our psyche and become visible on the level of consciousness. Take joy, for instance. The maturing Christian, while observing the exhiliration of joy in the newly "born again" Christian who has recently experienced a focal awakening of Christ within, may raise questions about his or her own lack of exuberance after years of loving communication and growing communion. What some fail to realize is that *peace* is the perfection of joy. It not only delivers the soul from the fretful trouble of exterior things but calms the inner fluctuations of its desires and in a marvelous way it unifies its affections. It makes the heart single in a triumphant love. Here, we find that after a period of cleansing, healing, freeing, unifying, there comes a time of centeredness in our growth center. It is a time when through the activity of the Holy Spirit we experience the delight of loving, the joy of communion, the tranquility of peace—a time of refreshment when we are bathed in glory. For what is important for us to remember is that the mature relationship now begun will continue for all eternity. Christ makes it clear that the relationship with him begun on earth will have continuity. "Eternal life is *knowing* thee." And what is significant here is the term "knowing," which in Hebrew means "intimate presence." For those concerned with life after death, the words from the living New Testament should take on a new meaning: "And in the end, your greatest glory will be that you belong to me" (2 Thess. 1:12).

That communion with God, which was broken in the Garden of Eden, is constantly being reestablished through his indwelling presence as we grow from communication to communion in our heavenly earthly abode, our growth center. There is a profound bond between this abode and the one which awaits us. (John 14:2-3). Through communion in this our earthly abode we are prepared for eternal life in the house of the Father. Thus in the discourse at the Last Supper Jesus assured us of his desire to be united to us and also of the continuity of this loving relationship, by establishing it with us while he was yet on earth.

Christians throughout the centuries have both experienced and taught this reality. It is part of our roots. This is what Christians who have an awareness of the indwelling personal presence of God will tell you. It is not a pious hope. As you grow in an inward relational faith from loving communication to intimate communion and become more sensitive and responsive to him, the Holy Spirit will "reveal God to you, . . . so that you will know what is the hope to which he has called you, how rich are his wonderful blessings . . . and how very great is his power at work in you" (Eph. 1:17-18).

In conclusion, the Christian growth experience which develops from communication to communion with God on the vertical level begins with a focal awakening as we mature from communication to communion in a loving intimacy with Christ within. On the horizontal level, as we will see, growth begins with forms of psychological togetherness and immature relationships which develop into agape communion and fellowship. As soon as Christian consciousness on the vertical level becomes a reality in your life, you become sensitive to the importance of a mature agape relationship with others, and your activated love-faith becomes prayer in action.

UNDERSTANDING MATURITY
as the experience of
GROWTH IN RELATIONAL FAITH
FROM
COMMUNICATION

Inward ———————————— *Toward*

GOD   ### FELLOWMAN

Experiencing: Experiencing:
a focal awakening   psychological bonds
                                of togetherness
a fleeting awareness of
God's presence   improved human dynamics

a "born-again" experience   committee associations
"baptism in the Spirit"   and procedures

Prayer: vocal and reflective   warm Christian relations

TO
COMMUNION

intimate communion   agape fellowship with Christ as
with God in your growth   the bond of unity in community
center

Prayer: wordless and contem-   Prayer: in the Holy Spirit with
plative   ministry to one another

AND
GROWTH IN AN ACTIVATED LOVE-FAITH
"Prayer in Action"
WITH

power to live and power to give
a blending of contemplation and action,
personal renewal and social renewal

Chapter V
Agape Consciousness

A new agape consciousness is developing today among Christians which reflects a deepening of relational faith beyond the dynamics of improved communication to a real communion in fellowship. There are many evidences of this trend not only within churches, but among churches Protestant and Catholic alike. Several years ago, at a conference on the Holy Spirit at Trinity Episcopal Church in New York, Cardinal Suenens noted that Christians today are communing at a deeper level. According to George Gallup, this is a matter of fact. An increasing number of people are experiencing a relationship with God and the people of God which reflects a maturing process not only within but between Christian groups. The quest for depth should be an interfaith quest as the eminent Presbyterian John Mackay prophetically points out:

> The most significant bond between the great Christian traditions is something all Christians need to pray for . . . to rediscover . . . to promote . . . namely the Life of God in the Souls of men . . . only then . . . will the quest for Christian unity move beyond appearance to Reality.[1]

Beyond Belief

Genuine agape fellowship as experienced by Christians today is beyond belief. It is beyond those systems of thought that have in the past divided so many Christians. You need not compromise your own views to have fellowship in love. You simply have to accept the other person as one loved by Christ. Evidence of Christians of all denominations praying together in agape love is constantly on the increase.

Today, the Protestant-Catholic experience of relational faith within prayer groups is becoming in many instances so heartfelt that it parallels the agape experience you read about in scripture. There is a sharing together at deep levels of prayer, ministry, and biblical insight. Those involved in small groups believe that this is where Christians should place their emphasis in a quest for unity—on the level of agape fellowship rather than the organizational level. Both, for the present, may be needed until all are inspired by a common bond of love in the Holy Spirit, reminiscent of Paul's words in 2 Thessalonians, "The love each of you has for the others is becoming greater" (1:3 GNB).

In agape fellowship it is not our heads but our hearts which we must bring together through the single attraction exercised by Christ. Without such a center there can be no true unity. The charismatic leader, the guru, the political official, can be no substitute for Christ; as unifying agents they are only human shadows of the Reality.

Those who think along Marxist lines have a degree of group communication, but no center of attraction. They are held together as if enclosed in a vault, or a closed circuit, by which

COMMUNION
IN AGAPE FELLOWSHIP

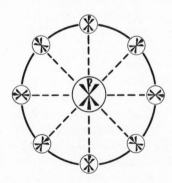

MARXIST: "CLOSED CIRCUIT
WITH NO CENTER OF UNITY"

they claim to achieve wholeness to the extent that they
participate in the system.

On the other hand, Christian fellowship in communion has a
center capable of inspiring, preserving, and releasing power,
and the ability to unify a host of earthly loves that in turn share
love with one another as the illustration shows.[2]

What is happening today was once described by the sixth
century spiritual writer St. Dorotheus of Gaza. He likened the
spokes of a wheel which are joined at the center to Christians
maturing in their relational faith; the nearer Christians come to
their center in Christ, the nearer they come to each other.

Agape Love Is Eternal

Max Thurian, a Calvinist monk of the monastery of Taizé,
insists that we should probe our spiritual roots in order to gain a
more mature understanding of relational faith in its eternal
dimension. We should seriously reconsider that ancient belief
contained in the Apostles Creed, "I believe in the communion
of saints." He attributes our present spiritual illiteracy on the
subject to a post-Reformation reaction against the extremes of
medieval piety. This seems to be another case of throwing the
wheat away with the chaff.

The pendulum of history has recently swung again to
exaggerations and "pieties" as starving Christians feed on the
husks of demonology and phenomenology. Why should
Christians become so absorbed in demons rather than

ministering angels? Why should Christians become so crazed about phenomena relating to life after death, and even look upon such phenomena as a major breakthrough in modern times? Didn't the pagan Greeks believe in immortality? How much more Christians have in the inner consciousness of their new love-life in the risen Christ which is eternal and which will continue in life after death, for as Paul says, love is eternal.

Besides the historic neglect of one aspect of our spiritual roots, how can we account for this misguided enthusiasm? Could it be just another case of mistaking appearances for reality, of being once more off-focus? Of giving attention to the outer rim of psychic consciousness instead of the inner circle of Christ-consciousness—the highest consciousness? It is time to pause and reflect.

In the first place, you will come to the realization that only those who are already experiencing an inward relational faith and an agape consciousness can in any way appreciate the more profound truths experienced in the communion of saints. Could not some of the misunderstandings of this great mystery, both past and present, be due to the immaturity of those who have interpreted it in terms of the human dynamics of communication rather than on the level of intimate communion and agape love?

Once you have experienced a deep inward-toward relational faith, the inner meaning of the communion of saints will take on new meaning. You will then want to probe further in your spiritual roots for the inner meaning of Christ's love as the bond between time and eternity. The inner meaning of his love not only unites us here and now in a new agape love, but with all who are in Christ in every age and place and extending to saints of all traditions.

In Heaven as on Earth

Only those who here and now enjoy a Christ-consciousness as well as an authentic experience of agape love can fully appreciate the communion of saints as found in the Apostles Creed. Agape communion requires a faith that works through love. It is based on a love shared in the spiritual realm. It reminds us of what Paul said:

> For I want very much to see you in order to share a spiritual blessing with you, to make you strong. What I mean is that both you and I will be helped at the same time, you by my faith and I by your faith. (Rom. 1:11-12 GNB)

If we are only now beginning to rediscover the meaning of communion in fellowship and ministry to one another, through the gifts of the Holy Spirit in agape prayer groups, it is understandable how the eternal aspect of this fellowship would be a total blank for most Christians. Yet it is easy to see that if the risen Christ is the source of love, the triumphant in Christ on earth would share his love as Christians interrelate with one another. Certainly, you can envision the triumph as so many members of an agape fellowship share their love and glory with each other eternally.

As you grow, your inward relational faith and agape consciousness will enhance your understanding of that love of others in Christ; that love which Paul says is eternal. You will have a deeper understanding not only of the agape relationships existing *among* the triumphant, but *between* the triumphant in Christ—the common source of love—and ourselves. For instance, God sends his ministering angels to help us realize we are all part of a great and noble family in love with one another through him. Love is not only eternal; love is the bond between time and eternity.

As you mature in a relational faith toward others growing from communication to communion in fellowship, the inner meaning of the eternal reality of the communion of saints will begin to unfold. If maturing Christians minister in love-power to one another, how much more will they be able to share his love when they reach maturity in eternity?

In an effort to understand the inner meaning of the

communion of saints, it is necessary to draw near to the one who
is the bond of love between time and eternity—Jesus. To draw
near to Jesus is to draw near to the heavenly Jerusalem, the
angels, and the saints. The presence of the angels and the saints
must be regarded in the light of John's doctrine of love of God,
a sharing, caring, love. We must examine the very nature of
love itself, for the ultimate miracle of Christianity is that the
risen life has been given us to share with one another in love.
This is the call of maturing Christians who can be agents of
renewal on the way to glory.

Prayer in Fellowship

Prayer centered in love is the most effective outreach. To
those who insist that we must constantly be doing something,
building something, reforming something, we need to raise the
question, "What if the doers do not have the energy to do?" For
if love-power is the most energizing force for genuine renewal,
it needs to be activated constantly through prayer. Often those
who lack superior talents and dramatic calls to go out on the
cutting edge of society provide prayer support for those who do.

Mature prayer fellowship is an area of ministry which as time
goes on will come under increasing scrutiny, chiefly because of
the many answers to prayers reported by maturing Christians in
agape prayer fellowship. These reports, which often involve a
precision in timing to equal similar stories passed down from
biblical times, may well challenge scientific evaluation in the
future. For instance, a professor at Princeton told me of a
remarkable sudden healing he had had when, following what
would otherwise have been a fatal accident, his wife called upon
a prayer group in Chicago for prayer ministry. Drawing on the
broader base of historical data, we know that the era of the
Fathers of the Desert, who were dedicated to prayer ministry,
coincided with an era of the flowering of Christianity far beyond
the desert.

Prayer Fellowship for Maturing Leaders

There should be creative types of prayer meetings for those whose tastes and needs vary. It should be noted here that those most in need of prayer fellowship and support often receive the least assistance. They are continually called upon to serve others, yet seldom receive any kind of supportive prayer fellowship. Among these are professionals, clergy, and community leaders, either unaccustomed to praying with their peers in an informal way or uncomfortable in the style of prayer meetings often available. They have also had their fill of dialogue and group dynamics. I had all this in mind several years ago while setting up prayer meetings for community leaders, pastors, and professional persons. I was concerned that the timing as well as the setting should be in harmony with their unique situation. The suggestions that follow are the result of these experiments and provide a program which could be adapted to other situations and settings.

Agape Fellowship—A Source of Vitality

A few directives

Invite a special resource person for the evening who has a background in a particular aspect of Christian consciousness, such as mature prayer forms. At one meeting we invited a Greek Orthodox Professor-Pastor who had been at Mt. Athos and was an authority on the Jesus Prayer. We also invited several other guests who had charisms of inner healing and were proficient in prayer ministry. Invite thirty people so that at least twenty will be able to make it the night that is convenient for your guest speaker. Either you or a friend can make a large attractive living room available for the evening and arrange it informally so that the guests will feel comfortable and can become acquainted easily.

A few reminders

Prior to the meeting remind the guests that its purpose is both informational and inspirational. A prayer fellowship should be renewing, supporting, and relaxing. Introduce your guest and allow thirty minutes for an informal presentation. Ask that the guests reserve their questions and comments until after the presentation.

A unique feature

After about twenty minutes announce a break. This can be an open time for fellowship or prayer with one or two of the persons present, or an opportunity to question the guest speaker personally. This informal approach will embarrass no one, particularly those unaccustomed to praying together; the first time some may care only to question the speaker. There may be others who are inclined to form groups of two or three for supportive prayer. This break also offers an opportunity for warm fellowship, coming as it does in the middle of the evening rather than the end when people often feel pressed to leave.

Renewing our heart and facing the earth

Following the break there is a reconvening for prayer to focus specifically on the concerns of the civic, social, and religious leaders present—prayers for the church, the community, the city. This is the high point of the evening, an opportunity to direct prayer power to persons involved in public life, including those present, and to matters of common concern to the group. Refreshments follow and then farewells.

A meeting such as this can be repeated, not necessarily restricted to the same people, but open to all who come at one time or another. This type of prayer fellowship is meant for busy persons and those who want to come and go as they please. A regular weekly meeting would be too demanding on the kinds of persons the group is meant to attract. Have a meeting when resources as well as participants are available.

Chapter VI
From Communication to Communion in Fellowship

Today, Christians with an inward relational faith are moving toward others in many varieties of groupings, or Christian fellowships, which show signs of nurturing the maturing process. There is evidence in many of these of a new Christ-consciousness, of a "faith that works through love" (Gal. 5:6) as it grows from communication to communion. Communion in fellowship, like communion with God, is the hallmark of a mature Christianity. And as we mature in our understanding of this great Christian mystery, we are reminded of those penetrating insights of Bonhoeffer, who wrote his doctoral dissertation on the communion of saints.[1]

He says that this community (communion of saints), which in history is never more than incipiently realized and is constantly breaking up, is indeed real and eternal. For in communion there is a revelation of one heart to another consummated in divine love. It is in the mutual revelation of hearts, filled by the Holy Spirit, that we experience a genuine agape community of love on the level of the new consciousness. In agape communion Christians find one another in him and flow together; the inward-vertical relationship with God cannot be separated from the horizontal relationship toward the neighbor. Both belong together. This is what communion in fellowship—agape love—is all about.

In other words, in Christ we have a common message point as we go back into a single center where we are at home with him and with one another through him. We begin to realize that he actively moves in all those who are docile to his will, suffusing them with his love, peace, and joy. The relationship of each of us to one another in Christ is a very real one; and moreover it is an eternal relationship. In him you have a power that goes deeper than democracy, where the bond is the will of the people, or church procedure, where Robert's Rules of Order reign supreme. Here the real center is a Person who is love, enabling the group to mature in relational love as it grows from communication to communion in fellowship.

This exceeds the humanistic approach to togetherness, which for so long has provided a social theory to which the church adhered. Few committees, today, resemble what communion in fellowship was like among the early Christians! The very existence of such a fellowship, other than among the Quakers, has until very recently been unknown to the average Christian. In the place of a Christ-conscious unity there have been less mature social theories which have provided the psychological and humanistic undergirdings for church activity. That inward relational faith of person to person in Christ—that precious agape communion—has been supplanted by increased interest in communication, or the horizontal relationship of person to person. To claim we must first love man and from there reach God is to pervert what John said in his First Epistle. It is God's love for us which is central. What is true is that the love we have for one another tells us if we love God.

For those who see in this trend a prod from God some will recognize that advances in psychology on the level of human relations can be placed at the service of the Spirit but are in no way a substitute for the reality of the Holy Spirit in Christian fellowship. He is the bond of unity and the source of vitality as Christians mature in communion with God and one another in an authentic agape relationship. One that begins with a Christ-consciousness within you as you reach out toward the other in a loving communication that eventually matures into a communion in fellowship.

Horizontal Communication:
Hazards and Growing Pains

There are hazards and growing pains in the maturing process of the Christian group just as there are with individuals whose focal faith with Christ at center is still weak. While the appearances of unity are present, the reality of Christian agape love is hardly visible in some cases or at best found in an immature form of communication often labeled Christian fellowship. Some problems of this situation are:

1. Commitment to the committee. Many religious people today are not over-committed but over-committeed; their time and energies are continually absorbed in a form of relationship (hardly fellowship) on a less mature level of communication. This tendency is due in part to a prevailing notion in America that religious and social progress is indeed achieved by committees, which in turn jerk civilization forward by a series of convulsions known as subcommittees. Some religious people seem perfectly satisfied with this immature form of relationship; while others are pacified by being told that they also serve who only wait on standing committees. They both have yet to experience agape Christian fellowship.

2. Slavery to procedure. This hazard involves making an idol of Robert's Rules of Order; becoming enmeshed in fine points of procedure; constantly hassling over who is to hold which position and role, all done with the benefit of a token opening and closing prayer.

3. Group pressure. Among the growing number of small prayer groups, as well as among other forms of group gatherings, a controlling religious clique manipulates others with "holy control." For the discerning participants, those groups sometimes resemble the Black Panthers, the difference being that in such cases you need reminding of those inalienable holy rights with which you are endowed by your Creator as expressed in the Declaration of Indepen-

dence, particularly, of the right to privacy, with which no group may tamper. For manipulators to "baptize" their procedures in the name of the Holy Spirit is a spiritual travesty. Authoritarianism is only one of the more insidious techniques used to penetrate and control the psyche of others in a group situation.

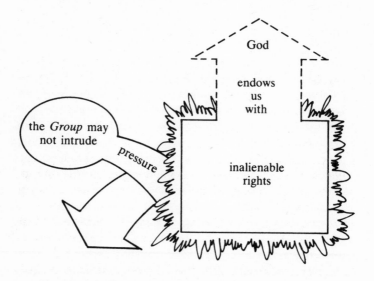

4. Naiveté. Assuming that what a group decides by majority vote or whatever is itself automatically right, without listening in prayer. If a group decides by majority vote to rob a bank, does that make it right? The work of the Holy Spirit in many cases is completely submerged as inspiration goes by the board. The situation reminds us of how David was pressured by a group of his soldiers to kill the sleeping Saul, which would have meant a clear victory for David. Instead, David followed God's inspiration and took Saul's cloak, a reminder to Saul of what he had really missed!
5. Group dynamics. While various forms of group dynamics

offer advantages over committee bickering, mechanistic procedures, and clique manipulation, these are at best immature forms of communication and togetherness. They are particularly hazardous when situations of forced intimacy are set up which often result merely in an exchange of negative hangups. On the other hand, there is no stopgap like the Holy Spirit and his divine healing power as is found in authentic Christian prayer fellowship.

6. Human relations groups. These are quite popular among Christians today who often assume you can find Christ in others without first finding him in yourself. How can you expect someone to find Christ in you (Gal. 5:16) if you have not found him yourself? While this is an improvement over the purely human dynamics of togetherness, this form of communication is still immature. However, it may well prompt disillusioned members to search further for a more mature form of relational faith toward others, and perhaps they will come across one of the numberless Christian groups, such as the charismatics, who are maturing in agape fellowship.

It is clear that this discussion is not addressed to the needs and problems per se of a worshiping community, but rather to other forms of Christian fellowship with which the average church-goer is already familiar. To disassociate yourself from a group because the ideal is as yet not real is like deciding not to drive a car because of accidents. At the same time you do need to ask yourself a few questions. Does this particular group enable me to mature in Christ? Does it in some way give me the support I need in a ministry to others? Am I, or will I be, in a position to integrate sufficiently with the group and its goals to be of personal assistance as it grows from an immature form of communication to a maturer agape fellowship centered in Christ? Is this the fellowship for me?

If your answers are negative, you may need to look elsewhere or pause to reconsider your understanding of the meaning of Christian fellowship itself. You may need reminding that to have a relational faith toward others, which is a maturing experience for all, does not necessarily mean relating in large numbers. Jesus said when *two or three* are gathered together in my name, I am in their midst. He didn't say twenty-three! So for the present you may find what you need in Christian fellowship with one or two prayer partners with whom you have planned your own ministry for maturity. As partners you can help each other in a supportive relational love to grow to the full stature of Christ.

On Earth as It Is in Heaven

When Christian fellowship grows beyond the level of communication, human dynamics, and togetherness to agape communion, you begin to understand the meaning of maturing in a relational faith toward others centered in conscious love of Him. You are not thinking here of two loves, human and divine, but of one love. Human love when taken hold of by the Holy Spirit becomes communion of the highest order with God and fellow humans. This is the essence of the Christian experience. There are not two loves, one heavenly and the other earthly; love is one sentiment with the difference that when human love is united to Christ it becomes infinite.

The distinction between natural and supernatural love is unnecessary; for what is found in natural love is not lost but is expressed in a more excellent way in divine love. In him alone can love of friend, spouse, parent, or child find fulfillment. And your natural love of others in agape relationship is an outgrowth of your love of Christ. This love is the highest of human experiences on earth as it is in heaven. Communion with God and with our fellows is like the last hue in a rainbow of human experience that begins with sense pleasures, intellectual satisfactions, enjoyment of the arts, then human love, and finally divine love in communion with God and others.

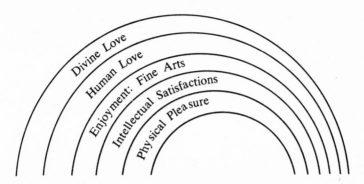

We can take courage from the fact that something is happening today in this new relational consciousness toward others in Christ that is reminiscent of what Thomas Kelly wrote some years ago. He said that in every period of profound rediscovery of God's love there is also a period of group-consciousness, of men and women knowing one another in him. This is truly happening today. Kelly points out that it appeared in vivid form among the early Friends and evangelicals; a deep inward relational faith flowing into a warm relational faith toward others.

The experience of God brings with it a bond of love and fellowship. While you may read about this bond, hear about it, or even experience it, one thing is completely certain, you cannot organize it! You don't deliberately create it simply because it is the work of the Holy Spirit who breathes where he will. This is an increasing realization among Christians today who are in incipient stages of becoming a communion of saints as they mature from loving communication with each other to authentic communion in fellowship. Thomas Kelly also comments that

the final grounds of holy fellowship are in God. Lives immersed and drowned in God are drowned in love and know one another in Him, and know one another in Love. God is the medium, the matrix, the focus.[2]

It is only when Christians have this divine bond of fellowship that they can effectively engage in a common effort for social renewal built upon the underlying foundation of authentic love and trust.

Once you mature beyond the dynamics of communication to an agape consciousness centered in Christ's love in you and in the group, you begin to realize that this agape experience like that of Christ in your growth center is a mature form of Christian consciousness. Agape fellowship provides strength and support to all who share the love of Christ with one another.

Chapter VII
An Activated Faith: Prayer in Action

Communion with God and the people of God opens your psyche to a new dimension of Christian consciousness. For as your faith becomes activated you experience the transforming effects of the Holy Spirit in your growth center. He begins to enrich your whole life. Problems, joys, and sufferings now become means of activating your faith and of generating love-power. You are maturing in a relational faith which works through love and provides strength under stress. Love is actually at the heart of social renewal; it flows from your continual inner renewal on the way to glory!

As you mature from communication to communion with God and with others, Christ becomes in you not only a living presence but a love-power. For what God did for man in and through Christ, he now begins to do in and through you. He meets you, communes with you, changes both you and the direction of your life. As you reach out to others in an activated faith, he empowers you to live and to give with ever-increasing effectiveness through the Holy Spirit. Here you may recall Paul's inspiring words.

> I ask that your minds may be opened to see his light, so that you will know what is the hope to which he has called you, how rich are the wonderful blessings he promises his people, and how very great is his power at work in us who believe. (Eph. 1:18-19 GNB)

As you mature in your inward relational faith, you become more conscious of that deep creative love by which you are being transformed into an agent of the Holy Spirit, a channel of his grace to others, a minister of his maturing love. You are in fact becoming part of the great human undertaking of bringing the whole world nearer to Christ. Your Christian consciousness expands into an activated faith, your natural gifts now enriched and enhanced by the Holy Spirit, prepare you for an effective outreach to those around you through social work, social action, and prayer ministry. For the experience of his intimate presence is an experience of deep peace, an experience not of inaction but of power to live and power to give. You no longer resemble those who "hold to the outward form of religion but reject its real power" (2 Tim. 3:5).

Through your activated faith you become a witness to the love-power of Christ within—the source of your vitality—and you are better able to live the gospel message in new and creative ways in tune with time and circumstance. Perhaps no better model of the mature Christian with a total receptivity and response to God's love can be found than in Mary, the mother of Jesus. But there are others. Evelyn Underhill writes of Catherine of Genoa that she came "bright faced from ecstasy, life's dreadful wrecks to tend, and for his sake acclaimed each a friend." To be a witness does not mean spreading propaganda or making an impression, but rather to live in such a way that your life would be unexplainable if God's love-power did not exist. Francis of Assisi, the most unspoilt channel of Christ's love since New Testament times, was such a witness. Through a unique love-faith activated by his prayer life, he was able to apply the gospel message in prophetic ways to the unusual circumstances of his day. Some today are called to do likewise and in the process to *make the good news—news.*

Secular humanists often fail to see the difference between a purely humanitarian outreach and one that is activated by a faith growing out of the love of the Holy Spirit within. For that matter, even project-oriented Christians, busy winning brownie-points for heaven and eager "to bring in the kingdom," fail to see the difference. Deeper even than human love is the fact of God's love, the fact of Jesus Christ. And here we touch the very heart of the Christian mystery. Deeper than our services and our ministries lies the reality of God's love in the Holy Spirit, who is the source of our power to live and to give. Christian consciousness includes the experience of this love-power.

Hazards, Snags, Obstacles

In any effort for good, whether in your own surroundings, in social work, social action, or prayer ministry, you will be faced with hazards, snags, and obstacles; and you will begin to realize that it is only through transcendent love that you have the power to overcome these problems and the strength to face all conditions by that power than Christ gives (Eph. 4:13). Gradually you will come to realize that this authentic source of energy will sustain you and enable you to bring your Christian efforts to final completion. Like Paul you will often be forced into complete reliance on Christ within your growth center, who makes power perfect in infirmity and in weakness gives you strength. A weakness that forces you to rely on him has its own advantages.

Bonhoeffer wrote from prison that modern man can cope with every danger except the danger of human nature itself. You will readily admit that there are many trying circumstances in life for which genius and talent alone are insufficient. To cope with these as a maturing Christian requires an activated faith, a strength and a Christian consciousness to which Paul refers in a letter to some early Christians groping for growth. He inquires, "Does your life in Christ make you strong? Does his love comfort you?" (Phil. 2:1).

The stress and strain of coping with difficulties and overcoming evil with good, as Christians are commanded to do, can lead to despondency and despair without the sustaining love of Christ. Left to fend for ourselves, sometimes working side by side with people who have little of the love of God in their hearts, we may readily yield to discouragement. Yet we should not be deterred, for we are called upon to reflect God's love and glory in a world of "crooked and mean people" as we "shine among them like stars lighting up the sky" (Phil. 2:15). The fact is that "he helps us in all our troubles, so that we are able to help those who have all kinds of trouble, using the same help that we ourselves have received from God. Just as we ourselves have a share in Christ's many sufferings, so also through Christ we share in his help" (2 Cor. 1:4-5).

Some situations call for another Francis to live out his motto, "Where there is hatred, let me sow love." To do this we need a strong activated faith centered in love with power to live and to give, and then we will realize the truth of those words of Paul, "Nothing can separate me from the love that is in Christ Jesus." "In all our troubles I am still full of courage. I am running over with joy" (2 Cor. 7:4).

In the same strain, Chardin says in *The Divine Milieu* that in Christ alone, as in a boundless abyss, our powers can launch forth into activity. In him we find relief from tension and the certainty that in his depths we will experience no wreck-rocks of failure, no shallows of pettiness, no currents of perverted truth.[1]

Just as the growth pattern for a relational faith cannot be fitted to a blueprint since the experience of this form of Christian consciousness differs with each individual, the same can be said of an activated faith. How does the love-power of the Holy Spirit operate in your life? Often, your natural gifts are enriched and enhanced, for "the kingdom of God does not consist in talk but in power" (1 Cor. 4:20). In some cases there is a complete moral transformation, in others a gift of contemplation, in others a gift of counseling and inner healing. The list is limitless. The timing of the unfolding of these gifts cannot be determined in advance. That same love with its freeing, healing, cleansing, unifying effects on a personal level providing you with power to live, operates on a social level in the many and varied gifts of ministry providing the power to give. The common denominator is the energizing love of the Holy Spirit.

PRAYER IN ACTION:
A Growth Experience

We shall become mature men reaching to the very height of Christ's full stature. (Eph. 4:13)

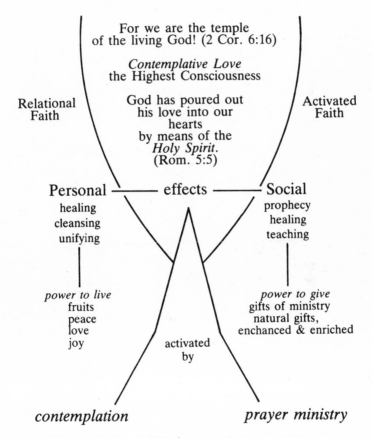

For we are the temple of the living God! (2 Cor. 6:16)

Contemplative Love the Highest Consciousness

God has poured out his love into our hearts by means of the *Holy Spirit.* (Rom. 5:5)

Relational Faith

Activated Faith

Personal ——— effects ——— Social

healing
cleansing
unifying

prophecy
healing
teaching

power to live
fruits
peace
love
joy

power to give
gifts of ministry
natural gifts,
enchanced & enriched

activated
by

contemplation

prayer ministry

spiritual communion
and
Holy Communion

Where the spirit of the Lord is present, there is freedom. (2 Cor. 3:17)

Does your life in Christ make you strong? Does his love comfort you? (Phil. 2:1)

Even though our physical being is gradually decaying, yet our spiritual being is renewed day by day. (2 Cor. 4:16)

The Spirit's presence is shown in some way in each person, for the good of all. (1 Cor. 12:7)

He has blessed us with every spiritual gift. (Eph. 1:3)

I ask that your minds may be opened . . . so that you will know . . . how very great is his power at work in us who believe. (Eph. 1:18-19)

Prayer in Action

As you mature in an activated faith as a way of life—prayer in action—how to relate your Christian consciousness to the world of action becomes a real challenge. On the level of ordinary consciousness, this matter was seen as just a question of organization. But now on the level of a new consciousness things are different.

As you begin to mature in an inward relational faith often a period of incubation sets in; it is frequently a time to slow down before you reach outward in an activated faith. The tension between prayer and action is very real, but just another growth experience. First you will feel inclined to spend time in contemplative prayer alone with Christ, contemplation being a time when you rest in him as he works in you. This early period of spiritual development, following a focal awakening, is a desert time when you are in a period of Christ-consciousness which is "quiet." At this time, you are like a child who needs the shelter and warmth of a home environment to grow to a healthy and wholesome maturity. You are not ready to be an adequate instrument in a major undertaking for social renewal. It is a time, as Teresa expresses it, when the "soul neither stirs nor moves and is rejoicing in the holy repose which belongs to Mary." As your relational faith matures outwardly into an activated faith, you will be able to put prayer to work, or contemplation to action, with a greater degree of ease and effectiveness.

It is at this point in your maturing process that service and action work harmoniously together, as Teresa expresses it, you can now be both Mary and Martha. As a matter of fact, it is only when you mature in love relationships that the tension of the less mature period of growth ceases. It is this growth-tension which seems to be the main problem. Although we need reminding that Jesus did not take exception to Martha's work so much as to her "busy-ness" about her work. He said to her, "You are busy about many things." What modern parallels could be drawn!

It is the gradual maturing of your inward relational love-faith that brings effectiveness to your outward activated faith. Jesus said, "I appointed you to go and bear much fruit, the kind of fruit that endures" (John 15:16). Teresa also speaks of this mature phase of prayer in action in *The Interior Castle*.

> How little one should think about resting if the Lord makes his special abode in the soul. For if the soul is much with Him . . . its whole thought will be concentrated on ways of pleasing Him and showing Him how it *loves* Him. . . . this is the aim of contemplation . . . of which are born good works . . . and good works alone.[2]

Christians through the centuries have tended to institutionalize their views on this matter. Liberal and evangelical Protestants as well as Catholic religious orders have stressed diverse life-style combinations of service and prayer. Individuals, however, have their unique personalities and growth patterns and in their quest for depth either get boxed in somewhere along the line or simply fail to identify with institutions for which they feel no personal affinity.

A ministry for maturity with spiritual counseling would enable such Christians, as they begin to grow in an activated faith, to realize that the tension they experience between prayer and action, before it becomes prayer in action, is simply part of the normal Christian growth experience.

Harvey Cox and other contemporary theologians are shedding new light on the relationship between the active and contemplative life, which has been a major issue with philosophers and religious thinkers for centuries. If you examine your roots, you will discover that the ancient Greeks attempted to grapple with this question of prayer in action. To them it was not a matter of a maturing process. They considered contemplation superior to action, and insisted, moreover, that action was simply an overflow of contemplation. Some today do not realize that this thinking actually influenced the early Fathers of the Church and later Thomas Aquinas and in turn more recent theologians and spiritual writers.

In the late nineteenth century, however, a young woman came along with a different understanding. This woman, known as Therese of Lisieux, was a Carmelite nun who died at the age of twenty-four. Theologian Hans Urs Von Balthasar maintains that she should be guaranteed a place in the history of theology because she was the first to rid contemplation of its ancient relics. She is the first to see, claims this eminent spokesman, that contemplation does not simply overflow into action. Her thesis is that both have their source in love and are equal. She preferred prayer to action because she considered it the most effective way of reaching others.

Many who have come into this new dimension of Christian consciousness, as it relates to an activated faith, experience a tension between prayer and action. Others who have matured through the years with the help of a sustaining life-style find that breakthroughs tend to resolve this tension almost instantaneously. This seems to have been the case with Dennis Bennett, well-known Episcopal charismatic, whose experience I described in an article in *Christian Century* based on a personal interview.

Q. Does the charismatic experience lead to a deeper prayer life? Does it resolve the "Martha-Mary" tension common to those seeking spiritual maturity?

A. When I was forty and a half, I found that I was drying up spiritually. I was putting out and taking little in. And I didn't know exactly what to look for. It was then that I met John and Joan, a young couple who had had a charismatic experience. Now, I have always longed to be a man of prayer—a longing that led me in all sorts of directions, from Quaker meetings to the writings of the great mystics; and I have had recurrent experiences of God's presence. A monastic friend once warned me: "You cannnot bring the mountain to the valley—you can't find God in the midst of noise." (Yet the New Testament is not a book of retreats; it shows us Paul going through life with a continual awareness in the midst of clamor.) Meeting John and Joan. I realized that they were then and there experiencing the warmth of God's presence, that they were on the mountaintop even while they were in the valley. The charismatic experience helps to bring this about. It is a release of the indwelling spirit, which arises and overwhelms the believer. The Lord comes out of the Holy of Holies to the outer court and then to the outer world. After sharing in prayer with John and Joan, I too felt this overflowing of the Spirit. I woke up next morning, and this tremendous sense of God's presence was still in me; and at noontime too it remained vivid.[3]

By reason of the charismatic renewal, we have more evidence today than formerly of the love of the Holy Spirit which overflows into action. While both prayer and action have their source in love, as indicated above, I would add that it is prayer and prayer ministry, as well as the sacraments, which activate the love that spills over into action. For this reason in some mysterious way prayer can be related to all forms of human endeavor, and even when we are not personally involved it triggers response!

As we reflect on this whole question of prayer in action, we begin to understand that it is a maturing process unique to each individual and largely associated with personal temperament and circumstance. Brother Lawrence experienced this form of Christian consciousness which remained with him during the most hectic circumstances. As already noted, gradual growth through a cocoon state is normal. For all, however, a sustaining life-style is a necessity: periods of solitude and silence, a desert experience, before moving out in the power of the Spirit. The trend today is to extend such periods beyond the usual weekend retreat in order to meet the demands and challenges of a mature Christian in today's world. The delightful allegory of Tryna Paulus, "Hope for the Flowers," furnishes profound insights on the question of prayer in action following a period of transforming cocoon growth.

While the question of prayer in action cannot be resolved on a theological level, it can be studied as part of the spiritual growth experience. It is not the ultimate in growth; it is only one aspect of it, as one continues to mature. In Dante's *Paradiso,* those who have attained this state are only midway in their triumphant ascent toward the life in glory. Prayer in action is a state of Christian consciousness, when, like a burning taper, you bring Christ's love to others, and each in turn shares it with another until the whole world is ablaze. It is a growth experience in another dimension of Christian consciousness when the Holy Spirit provides us with power to live and power to give. In conclusion, prayer in action is simply an outreach toward others through a love activated in prayer.

Prayer in Action

To describe prayer in action without noting how it becomes a way of life is like reviewing a seed catalogue without going

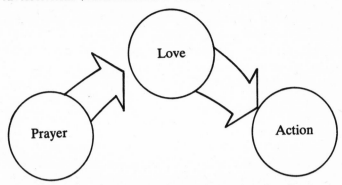

into gardening. While the blending of prayer and action is part of the spiritual growth process, supportive habits are important too. For instance, the prayer of breathing, as described in the following chapter, activates the love of the Holy Spirit that overflows into action. The prayer of referral, as we will see, feeds that love-faith within, making everything in life a means of growth, a sacramental. Another prayer form which relates directly to prayer in action is the listening prayer which prompts you to seek first the kingdom of God in all you do, sifting the chaff from the wheat, discerning appearances from reality, and developing a strong focal faith.

An important guideline to keep in mind as prayer in action becomes a way of life is to avoid attachment to the success and the results of your actions. This is difficult; its application points to maturity. Success or failure cannot be the determinant of worth. Regardless, however, benefits will accrue from your good actions activated by love through prayer. There will always be a deepening relationship with Christ, an increased amount of self-knowledge, an inner strength and peace as well as unexpected offshoots of what may have succeeded or failed. All in all, we must perform our actions quietly and reflectively, and for our constant personal guidance we must have an understanding of prayer in action as "a ruling sense of God's presence"!

Chapter VIII
Breathing a Prayer

Prayer in action is both a growth experience and a way of life, one that requires that each day become a sabbath by simply relating prayer with breathing and breathing with doing. The first thing to notice about God's activity on the sabbath is that it focuses on breathing. While a sabbath itself, as Harvey Cox suggests, is an answer to the profound question of the relationship between being and doing, sabbath also suggests a deeper form of spiritual consciousness. The spirit of the sabbath does not mean just a day for doing nothing, but rather a particular form of consciousness. A consciousness with which we all should identify if we hope to be God's instruments in renewing the earth. For as John White points out, it is only through a change of consciousness that the world will be saved. We must begin with ourselves. Moreover, all activity is futile, whether it be social work, political action, this-ism, that-ology, unless accompanied by a new and elevated mode of awareness. Where does one begin? With the prayer of breathing.

Breathing a prayer is not only another way to nurture maturity in your growth center, but a form of prayer in action. Do not regard the expression "to breathe a prayer" as just a literary form. It should be taken literally! Breathing a prayer is an easy way to keep in touch with your growth center. It is especially helpful if you are desiring to keep in touch with your center in the midst of a busy life. This desire in itself is an indication that you are maturing. The idea of breathing a prayer has already been mentioned in relation to the prayer of referral and the prayer-carrier or breather. Making a habit of this form of prayer will greatly simplify the prayer of referral for the maturing Christian. Breathing a prayer brings you in touch with the living flame and is a response to Paul's injunction that we "stir up the Spirit" within us. It is a gentle means of activating as well as responding to his love.

In *The New Man,* Thomas Merton says that the Holy Spirit comes to set the whole house of our soul in order, to deliver our minds from immaturity, fear, and prejudice. The question is, How do we cooperate? Thomas Kelly suggests that we should not exaggerate the difficulty of our response to the love of God within. We can have a very busy day outwardly speaking and yet be steadily in the holy Presence. It doesn't take time or complicated words of praise and adoration, it is simply a matter of a prayer that can be breathed all through the day.

> I should like to be mercilessly drastic in uncovering any sham pretense of being wholly devoted to the inner holy Presence, in singleness of love to God. But I must confess that it doesn't take time, or complicate your program. I find that a life of little whispered words of adoration, of praise, of prayer, of worship, can be breathed all through the day. One can have a very busy day, outwardly speaking, and yet be steadily in the holy Presence.[1]

Breathing a prayer brings Christian mystery and experience together. It is scripture coming alive in you. What could be more biblical than God's breath in you? And what more sublime way for you to respond to the sacredness of his love than breathing? Breathing a prayer is an approach to prayer suited to all stages of your life. In the beginning it will enable you to establish yourself in a simple but deep form of prayer beyond reflection, and later on it will help you in a habitual way to yield to the work of the Holy Spirit in your growth center.

In relation to the prayer of referral, breathing can become a prayer-carrier as you waft with a breath whatever fuel you have into the living flame of love in your growth center.

Finally, this approach, once it becomes part of you, will be at your disposal in dire circumstances, when words fail! And here we are reminded of that desire expressed by Chardin, in "The Hymn to the Universe," that his last breath would be a breathing prayer, a breath of communion with the living God. All of this is in Genesis! "Then he breathed into his nostrils a breath of life and thus man became a living being" (2:7). And Genesis can become a living reality in our lives, because when we breathe a prayer, God breathes his very own life into us. As a maturing Christian you can find this prayer a way of keeping continually in touch with God by simply breathing.

New Testament writers describe religious consciousness in terms of breathings of the Holy Spirit. Breathing a prayer keeps you in harmony with the Holy Spirit in your growth center. It is a mode of preparing his way as well as responding to him. The Holy Spirit can move through you to the degree of your openness and readiness. You may be like a car that allows gas to flow through its engine as it speeds rhythmically on its way. Or you may be like a car in which high-test gas can do little good because it is sputtering around in need of a tuneup.

There are a number of advantages to breathing a prayer. (1) First of all it will enable you to blend your active life with your prayer life more readily and thus resolve on the level of living what theologians attempt to resolve on the level of theory—the tension between prayer and action, which now becomes prayer in action! (2) Through its use the Spirit becomes more active in your growth center, and your life will be enriched and sustained as you move into a deeper prayer life. Breathing a prayer can keep you in touch with your growth center as you order your life on more than one level. On one level you can be thinking, discussing, seeing, calculating, and meeting all the demands of external affairs, but deep within, at a profounder level, you can be in prayer and adoration, song and worship, in gentle receptivity to the living breathings of the Holy Spirit in your growth center.

The world values activity on the first level, assured that this is where the real business of mankind is done. It only tolerates the cultivation of the second level. But in the society of the future all will know that quiet strength in their growth centers as they breathe in unison with the Spirit of God. The soul that breathes with God in his or her growth center will have vitality from this source of life. Evelyn Underhill notes that the citizen who is so strengthened is one whose roots strike deep into eternity; and as a result, his work is better, his judgment saner; his ability to bear pain, trial, and suspense is enormously enhanced.

You can keep in touch with your growth center by simply breathing! The separation between God and man is gradually broken as the Holy Spirit breathes his life into you day by day. After years of deepening faith and purification God's breath becomes one with your breathing.

This mode of expanded awareness is beautifully described by John of the Cross in extraordinary passages in the *Living Flame of Love*. He says that no knowledge or power can explain how it happens except by saying that the Son of God attained and merited such a high state for us, the power to become children of God (John 1:12). He further remarks that we should not think it impossible that the soul be capable of so sublime an activity as "this breathing in God, through participation, as God breathes in us."

John claims that this breathing from God to the soul and from the soul to God with frequency and love was actually what St. Paul meant when he said, "Since you are sons of God, God sent the Spirit of his Son into your hearts, the Spirit who calls to the Father" (Gal. 4:6). This passage, he affirms, applies not only to the blessed in the next life but to the mature Christian in this life! Such an experience, he says, is delicate, sublime, and indescribable, and what is most important to note—for those who live by logic and reasoning alone—is that it is beyond the grasp of the intellect![2]

Maturing Through Breathing

In the advanced stages of the maturing process, the experience of God's power is as gentle as that described in Luke

1:35 when the Holy Spirit "rested" on Mary, "overshadowed" Mary.

The experience of the breath of the Holy Spirit in your growth center, as an expansion of consciousness, often begins in the earlier stages of the maturing process; as you move to greater depth in the later stages of growth, the experience is one of deep communion with God. John says that as the breath of the Holy Spirit renews the soul with his breathings, he is preparing us for the coming of the Son of God. John likens the consciousness of God's breath to experiencing a life of love and glory.

> And in your sweet breathing
> Filled with good and Glory
> How tenderly you swell my heart
> with love.[3]

Nurturing Life in Your Growth Center

Breathing can be a prayer that is like singing praises to God. It is returning to God in a sublime and dedicated way man's precious gift of breath. To develop this habit—which can integrate your whole life—take a few minutes alone each day in breathing a prayer.

In some of the earlier habit-forming stages as you accustom yourself to breathing a prayer like the Jesus Prayer you will discover that breathing a prayer becomes a breather prayer, or prayer-carrier, in conveying the fuel of everything in life to the living flame of love in your growth center. As you breathe the name of Jesus or the Doxology:

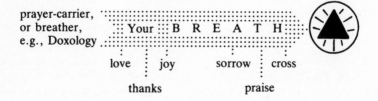

prayer-carrier, or breather, e.g., Doxology

Your B R E A T H

love joy   sorrow cross

thanks   praise

Breathing a prayer, as indicated earlier, can become a way of life which bridges the gap between your prayer life and your life of action. It can also be a maturing experience in that you will grow from loving communication to intimate communion, from vocal reflective prayer to the wordless prayer of love and intimacy, and from intimacy to power.

The Breath of the Holy Spirit in the life of a mature Christian can become a living experience. To acquire habits—which will stand you in good stead, at any time, in any place—the following exercise can be used.

1. Invoke the Holy Spirit as you sit still on a padded chair, not too high or low, with your back straight, head and neck erect, feet touching the floor, your hands held loosely in your lap, palms upward, your face, forehead, eyes, mouth, jaw relaxed. Be as little aware of your body as possible, leaving your soul free. Praise God and thank him for all he has done during the day.

2. Reflect for a moment on a passage of scripture. "As God himself has said, 'I will make my home with thee' " (2 Cor. 6:16).

3. Then concentrate your consciousness on the loving presence of Christ within your growth center. Remain in a profound loving act of adoration, lost in him. Exclude other thoughts, desires, sense perceptions (hearing, feeling, seeing).

4. Breathe deeply and rhythmically, since this in itself brings calm and peace.

   a. Inhale. Breathe through expanded nostrils; fill the area below the stomach—front, back, and sides—then fill the chest without raising the shoulders.

   b. Exhale. Do this through expanded nostrils, draw abdomen inward, exert diaphragm upward, slowly forcing breath upward; finally empty the chest without letting it sink.

   c. Pause to rest. Relax muscles of breathing.

   d. As you sink deeper into your growth center, use the

name of Jesus: "Jesus heal me," "Jesus free me," "Jesus save me," "Jesus bless them," "Thank you Jesus," "Praise you Jesus," etc.

e. Or if you want to use a breather, select a phrase from your favorite prayer or the Doxology, as suggested under the prayer of referral, and breathe the phrase rhythmically.

When breathing a prayer becomes a habit, it offers a simple prayer life which will support you as you mature from communication to communion in your growth center. Many ejaculations can be adapted to breathing and in a sense used as mantras.

SCRIPTURAL MANTRAS
LITURGICAL MANTRAS

1. Lamb of God, you take away the sins of the world, have mercy on us.

   Lamb of God, you take away the sins of the world, grant us peace.

2. Glory be to the Father, and to the Son, and to the Holy Spirit; as it was in the beginning, is now and ever shall be, world without end. Amen.

3. All my heart goes out to thee, O Lord my God (Psalm 25:1).

4. Hide me under the shelter of your wings (Psalm 17:8).

5. Blessed are you, O Lord, teach me to know your will (Psalm 119:12).

6. Peace I leave with you, my peace I give unto you (John 14:27).

7. Ah, how good is the good God. (Ah! Qu'il est bon le bon Dieu.) Julie Billiart

8. Lord Jesus, Son of the living God, have mercy on me a sinner!

9. A reminder of the potency of the prayer of breathing in times of crisis. "He shall kill Satan with his breath." What more could be said!

Chapter IX
From Inner Renewal to Social Renewal

Those who mature in an inward relational faith and experience its cleansing and healing effects on the human psyche are the first to admit that social renewal begins in our growth centers. Carl Jung once said that if individuals are not truly regenerated in spirit, neither can society be renewed since society is the sum of individuals in need of redemption.

Jacques Maritain claims that in man's efforts to renew society he should first begin "to purify the springs of history in his own heart." He insists that the roots of democracy are evangelical and spring from the hidden stimulation of the work of Christ within it, and of course within each Christian. On this same note, Douglas Steere says that as the saint finds his life laid open before the All Loving One, he is acutely aware that all the sins of society are present within his own heart. To change society, humankind must begin within. Those maturing in an activated faith are at the very heart of social renewal, since it is through our union with Christ that we have been created for a life of good works (Eph. 2:10). We must recognize that the betterment of the material conditions of life and the progress of science and technology will not be truly good for man unless placed at the service of those who know how to love.

Donald Bloesch says in the *Evangelical Renaissance* that the evangelism developing today, which places an accent on rebirth, is making an effort to relate inward change of heart to the social situation. He insists, however, that while individual conversion is the precondition for revolutionary social change,

101

of itself it is not sufficient to effect social change. It must be supplemented by social involvement.

A good example of social involvement, among thousands, are those Pentecostals in South America whose lives are activated by the indwelling Holy Spirit as they reach outward in a loving faith relationship to those in misery. In Chile, they are having great success in bringing men and women in the barrios to a fervent, committed Christian life. This, then, is an example of social renewal and transformation taking place as a consequence of inner renewal. The same is true in Brazil where economic stability has, in some instances, developed among the oppressed as a direct result of an activated faith experience.

George Cornell, an Associated Press religion editor, observed recently that today theologians are stressing anew that an activated faith with strengthened inner resources is essential to clarity of direction amid the world's muddled motivations. Christian leaders and leaveners of the future will be recognized by their activated faith-consciousness which brings with it a unique power to live and to give—a fortitude, growing out of an inner focus, or consciousness, centered in love with Christ in their growth centers.

In their quest for depth and maturity Christians will experience a continued death to life growth process, leading not only to personal but to social resurrection. In this regard Mark Hatfield observes that we have to have an inner vitality, we must continually allow ourselves to be transformed by Jesus Christ into messengers of reconciliation and peace, as we give our lives over to the power of his love. It is only then that we can soothe the wounds of war and renew the face of the earth and all humankind.

We may well raise the issue that we cannot wait until all hearts are renewed. We cannot allow one field to lie completely fallow and rely entirely on another one for new crops or destroy an old track before a new one has been completed. Dennis Bennett, in the same interview mentioned earlier, told me how the charismatic renewal, with its emphasis on personal renewal, is having an effect on social change. When I asked him if this movement was an example of social change based on personal renewal, he replied:

In a way, yes. Some say, "Don't do anything until human hearts change," but meanwhile civilization could go down the drain. While laws can lead to confusion until something changes inside, laws can hold the line until individual corrections are made. Ultimately, though, you cannot change society until the human heart is changed. One striking instance of this is the renewal of millions in Indonesia through a strong charismatic Christianity. In Indonesia, Muslims and communists—representing respectively what might be regarded as the establishment and the "new thing"—had long been fighting each other, with a charismatic Christianity in the middle. Now, because they have experienced this wonderful kind of Christianity, millions of Muslims and communists are becoming Christians. So breaches in Indonesian society are being sealed. The unique factor in social change is that the agents of change are individuals who not only have been converted but are receiving the equipment, the power, that makes them effective in social renewal.

But this sort of thing happens in other unlikely places too. Not long ago a parolee from San Quentin told me: "Father Bennett, you can't believe what is happening there. The charismatic movement is really taking over. You go into the prison yard and there are clumps of prisoners gathered around praying sanctimoniously. When they see another convict coming along they'll say, 'Hey, buddy, come over here and get straightened out!' They are ministering to one another. The parole board said to me: 'You are totally different; your whole personality has changed; there is no reason to keep you in prison.' " Certainly, such developments in personal reform should lead to prison reform.[1]

Fortunately, we need not theorize about what should happen—how a mature Christian should be an instrument in bringing about a mature society—we can be encouraged by the fact that it is already happening. In a recent speech George Gallup observed that

the really exciting news from our survey is that intrinsically religious people . . . those who truly live their faith—reinvigorate society far more than those who are extrinsically religious . . . those who are religious for social reasons and who are drawn to the church as an institution rather than to the church as an expression of God's love.

Evelyn Underhill says that the cultivation of the spiritual faculties is a "patriotic duty" and that the citizen strengthened by recourse to the inner source of vitality is worth more to the state than the person whose roots do not strike deep into eternity.

We must put on the mind of Christ and see the world and our involvement in it in relation to the Kingdom. We must first find God who reveals the world to us. To discover the world and God through the world is *less mature*. According to Paul, as Christians we are judges of everything yet judged by no man. Jacques Ellul points out that Christians have the gospel as their starting point. We do not have to base our decisions on current events, the news media, or react to everything that happens. We must constantly return to our roots; we do not have to find ourselves in relation to the social-political scene. Rather, the reverse action is the true one—we should give meaning to events; we should evaluate all in reference to God's glory and his kingdom both within and without.

We can look to the early Christians for some insight on this matter. Tugwell notes that they did not allow the world to determine their understanding of life, nor did they look for meaning in the prejudices of men. They had left behind the security of belonging to their age, of being men of their time. They became the bearers of different needs, goals, and satisfactions. They let Christ transform them; they abandoned the world of darkness in favor of the wonderful light in Christ. They lived in a spirit of freedom. This same victorious attitude not only applies to the political scene but should likewise apply to the decision-making process whenever and wherever we become involved in it, be it in a personal community or a church context.

Thomas Kelly takes us one step beyond Ellul. Although churches today often vie with corporations in their reliance on procedural niceties and rational decision-making, Kelly insists that a majority vote never indicates the right or wrong of a situation, rather it is the power of the presence of God which spells victory. In view of this we may be able to bring the light of the Holy Spirit into the decision-making process as it relates to our own personal life-style as well as our social involvements. In this way, we can become part of the process of inner renewal as it relates to social renewal.

Personal Decision-Making: Learning to Listen

If we personally wish to be instruments of social renewal, we must convert our growth center into a listening center. A center to which we frequently refer our attitudes and decisions to Christ within and allow our views and judgments to be shaped by his Holy Spirit. The prayer of listening is meant for the maturing Christian when seeking God's will in situations not so much involving ethical behavior as the making of wise choices between what is in the better or best interest of the kingdom of God.

As we mature in a Christian consciousness through the work of the Holy Spirit within, it becomes possible to "hear" more clearly God's loving communications. Listening includes response, without which prayer and contemplation are meaningless. To be fruitful, listening must not be isolated from life nor our living situation. In fact, it can blend a life of prayer with action.

The essence of the prayer of listening is finding God at the center of our soul as we develop a relationship with him in deep love and peace. It is then possible in this inner peace to sort out disturbing spirits of agitation, interior moods, and note their possible causes. Disturbance is often from the evil one. Listening enables us to discover the blocks which prevent us from growing and to seek the strength to overcome these. It means giving him our unsolvable problems to resolve.

In the prayer of listening the basic questions to resolve are:

How does this decision relate to the glory of God and foster the kingdom of God in others? How can it help us to mature to the full stature of Christ in communion with God and communion in fellowship? Perhaps this may sound too ideal. But our theme here is not how to begin but how to mature! Have we been content to settle for less? If so, we should replace our secular standards with gospel standards by learning what pleases the Lord (Eph. 5:10) and finding out what the Lord wants us to do (Eph. 5:17).

We must always be mindful of the fact that this world is not our home. He is our home. In the prayer of listening, we listen in solitude and quiet as he calls us to move into a more intimate relationship with him at the center, at the hearth of our home.

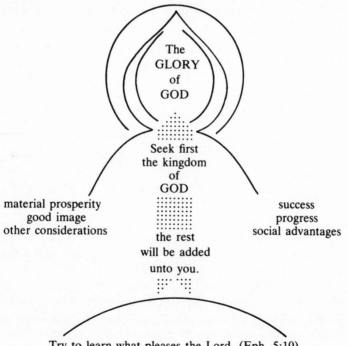

Try to learn what pleases the Lord. (Eph. 5:10)

The purpose then of the prayer of listening is to become ever more sensitive to his call, to cultivate a discerning heart, to strive for wisdom and understanding (I Kings 3:9-12), to nurture and activate the gift of counsel with which we were endowed at baptism. The Lord will then help us to make wise decisions as we enable others to do the same.

"Waiting for God"

It is better to wait for God, as Simone Weil so beautifully puts it, to pray through each step of the way, if we want to behave maturely. Spiritual adolescence is characterized by self-sufficiency. Prompt action is not always the best action. Prayer preceding action gives clarity as well as sustaining love-power to follow through. Thomas Carlisle writes:

Subpoena

Being subpoenaed
for prayer
is no punishment
but it is
an interruption
a postponement
for certain practical
considerations.

When God wants
us to wait
it is worth
devaluing
punctuality
in favor of
the charisma
of clarity.[2]

We need the strength of silence and the simplicity of love coming from our inner growth center to keep us free from confusion and to enable us to listen to the voice of God and the secret promptings of his love in perfect freedom, for God gives

complete freedom to those who are his. To seek God perfectly
we should refer our worldly anxieties to him in our growth
center, withdraw from the works that God does not want, and
from a glory that is only human display. It means that we
endeavor to keep our minds free from confusion by
entertaining silence in our hearts and listening for the voice of
God in order that our liberty may always be at the disposal of
his will. Thus we begin to cultivate an intellectual freedom
from the images of created things in order to receive the secret
contact of God in obscure love.

An Approach to the Prayer of Listening

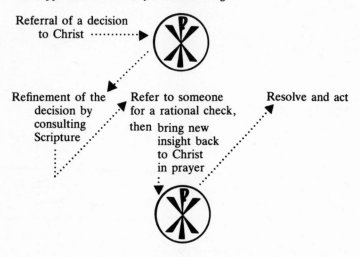

Head and Heart Decisions

With our roots and foundations in love and at home with
Christ in our growth center, we will be strong in our decisions.
Decisions involve both head and heart and must be made in
quiet silence. Calls for service accepted on the basis of
"heady" decisions alone often lead us into a dither. Thomas
Kelly insists that tension and rush are breeding grounds for

alien spirits. The Holy Spirit never leads us into situations of "panting feverishness." He says that when we say yes or no on the basis of inner guidance and whispered promptings of encouragement from our growth center, or even on the basis of a lack of it, we have no reasons to give except one—the will of God as we discern it. For when the will of God is the basis of our decisions we have begun to live in guidance. God never guides us into an intolerable scramble. After all he is at work in the world. It is not we alone who must frantically finish a task to be offered to God. Life from the center, Kelly insists, is one of unhurried peace and power. It is simple. It is serene. It is amazing. It is triumphant. It is radiant. It takes no time, but it occupies all our time. It makes our programs new and overcoming. We need not get frantic. He is at the helm. And when our little day is done we lie down quietly in peace, for all is well.

A Few Insights About the Prayer of Listening

Just because a cause is religious is not a mandate to get involved. Bear in mind that Jesus confined his efforts to Palestine while Rome was going to rack and ruin. The greatest need at any time is for maturing Christians to be still and listen. With our roots and foundations in love, we can begin to sort things out. Another approach to listening includes the following steps:

a) Gather evidence on the question at hand. This may involve a choice between two goods. (For instance, How best can I use my free time?) Ask, At this point in my life what is God's will for me?

b) Refer to scripture. In Hebrews, for instance, you will find how important it is to rest in God. This would support you in a decision to spend some time each Sunday in contemplation—to rest in him as he works in you.

    c) Ask yourself which decision brings harmony and peace. Then give your choice a dry-run, a short trial period.

    d) Next consult someone for further insight and guidance, always being alert to signs of confirmation pointing to the direction you should take.

    e) Be aware of circumstances in your life which favor or oppose a particular choice.

    f) Recognize that common sense is a "must" in any decision of the maturing Christian.

As we learn to listen to the Holy Spirit, we will be better able to consider such questions as: "How can I grow in a deeper relationship and communion with God?" "How can I more effectively use the natural gifts with which I have been endowed, not for myself alone, but for his greater honor and glory?" "How can I use the spiritual gifts, that is, natural abilities enhanced by the power of the Holy Spirit—gifts of ministry—given me for the benefit of God's people?"

It may be our responsibility to help others to pray through a situation which requires listening, rather than plunging ahead, and to support another with prayer and encouragement once a decision has been made. In a ministry for maturity we can become an instrument of that social renewal that comes from inner renewal. We can learn to listen rather than become an energetic operator, a self-sufficient religionist in a competitive age. We can counsel and encourage others to let God work through them as they mature in an ever-deepening relationship with him. Once again Thomas Kelly reminds us that our task is to call men to be still and know, to listen and hearken in quiet invitation to the subtle promptings of the Divine. Our first task is to encourage others to let go, to cease striving, to give over the fevered effort of the self-sufficient religionist trying to please an external deity, and instead to count on God knocking on the doors of time. "Behold, I stand at the door and knock." God is the Seeker, and not we alone; he is anxious to fill our time with a sense of presence. Religious people do not sufficiently count on God as active in the affairs of the world. Too many well-intentioned people are so preoccupied with the clatter of effort to do something *for* God that they don't hear him asking that he might do something *through* them. We may admire the heaven-scaling desires of the tower-builders on the Plain of Shinar, but they would have done better to listen and not drown out the call from heaven with the clang of the mason's trowel and the creaking of the scaffolding.[3]

Prayer counselors often meet with people who insist that service itself is prayer. Many of these are energetic people who project their dross on others rather than commune in relationships of authentic agape love. In order to be effective, the Christian must clearly begin within and integrate life around the central reality of God's love and presence.

Suggested Daily Form of Listening

1. Place yourself in the presence of God. Ask the Holy Spirit for light. Then bring to mind these questions: How has the Lord been working in my life lately? Thank him. Raise the questions: What is he now asking of me? What are some matters which need to be resolved with his help? Pause then to listen.
2. After reflecting on the areas of life which need to be changed, give attention to only one area, especially one which calls for conversion.
3. At this point use the prayer of referral, placing your concern for the matter which needs changing with him. Ask for healing, cleansing, and renewing.
4. If it surfaces that you have hurt someone or someone has hurt you, use the prayer of blessing.
5. Next offer a prayer of thanksgiving and praise for all he is doing in your life, for the Christian heart should always be filled with thanksgiving. The Doxology is often chosen as the expression of thanksgiving and used on a regular basis.

6. Now give attention to practical ways to respond to the guidance you have received in the area of your life you hope will be renewed as you continue to listen to the Holy Spirit.

Social Decision-Making

Once again, if we are to become more effective as instruments of renewal in the church and community at large, we must call upon the guidance of the Holy Spirit in our decision-making in order to discern *reality* from *appearance*. Many current decision-making practices used by religious organizations allow little latitude for the operation of the Holy Spirit. We must be open to his inspirations, freed from our own prejudices and also those immature social idolatries which deter us from furthering God's kingdom.

Inspired by Mackay's observation that the renewed life should express itself in creative action, I was prompted to develop a decision-making procedure which I have tested in seminars at Princeton Theological Seminary's Department of Continuing Education. The following procedure combines the rules of spiritual discernment with the techniques of creative problem-solving. It can prove helpful as a mature decision-making process to bridge the gap between prayer and action as well as a maturing experience for participants.

Creative Discernment

In a way, discernment is spiritual revelation; it enables us to discern the different types of spirits—human, divine, demonic—in a situation. It is a means whereby God makes us aware of what is happening. It differs from the usual approach to decision-making, which often elicits solutions mainly in terms of what we want, what the group wants, what the people we represent want, and not necessarily what God wants. This approach is especially suited to meetings in which Christians are seeking God's will for their church, community, etc.

General Principles

1. Ordinarily peace is from God. Disturbance, darkness, oppression, and confusion are from Satan.
   a. It therefore follows that decisions should not be made when the latter conditions prevail.
   b. It also follows that peace in the beginning and through to the end of the deciding process is a safe indication of a wise decision.
2. The relationship of a decision to the glory of God and his kingdom should be considered foremost.
3. The decision should agree with scripture.

Steps for Discernment

The above principles should be kept in mind while applying the following steps for discernment:
1. Pray for light in the group.
2. Collect options through the creative problem-solving procedure.
3. Then give personal prayerful attention to these options by:
   a) dialoguing with someone.
   b) regarding peace as the deciding factor.
   c) keeping God's glory foremost.
   d) checking scripture.
4. In the group seek confirmation with others by sharing the fruits of your insights and freeing yourself to experience peace through prayer.
5. Plan decisions for action with the understanding that these are open to further verification in lived experience, inner liberty, and enlightenment.

A Christian Decision-Making Procedure

Special steps for the meeting

1. The leaders and coleaders meet with the chairperson and begin by asking the Holy Spirit for guidance. The

chairperson then gives instructions regarding procedures and goes over the rules of discernment.

2. Immediately afterwards, the leaders assemble with the total group and give out information regarding:
   a) The rules of discernment
   b) Creative problem-solving procedure
   c) How the two can be interwoven in the decision-making process
3. The next session likewise opens with a prayer asking the Holy Spirit for guidance. The specific problem is then identified and clarified, and the rules for creative thinking explained.
4. The first stage is devoted entirely to the spontaneous listing of creative ideas to solve the problem at hand keeping in mind two basic rules: a) the more ideas the better and b) absolutely no criticism.
5. These ideas are listed on a tear sheet chart by the chairperson with the assistance of a coleader, while participants make their own lists.
6. After eight or ten minutes of creative idea-gathering, the chairperson asks the group to establish its own norms—five or six at most—for evaluating the ideas. For example, workability, cost, etc. At this point the process may be made distinctly Christian by the inclusion of norms related to fostering the kingdom of God. For example, does the decision foster Christian maturity, God's glory, or the gospel message?
7. The participants are asked to select five ideas from their own lists. Then they are to evaluate these ideas using a rating scale of 1 to 4—excellent, good, mediocre, poor—on their own evaluation sheets. After a few minutes the results are reported to the chairperson who records the averages on the tear sheet chart.
8. The chairperson then determines the top three or four ideas on a separate sheet and calls for a break. This allows the participants time to ponder over a final choice,

whether in prayer in the chapel, in a quiet room, alone, or with another person. This is also a time for applying privately the steps for discernment.

9. About thirty minutes later the participants reconvene and share their insights. The chairperson then reviews and applies the steps for discernment, following with group prayer and a final sharing of insights.

10. Now by a show of hands the group indicates what their final choice and the decision is. The meeting closes with a prayer of thanksgiving.

Creative Problem-Solving Procedure
(sample participant worksheet*)

I. Rules for Creative Thinking

1. Share any insights on the subject at hand. Criticism is ruled out.
2. All ideas are welcome. Even those which may seem ridiculous. (The "way-out" suggestions release tension and trigger thought.)
3. The more ideas the better. The faster they come the better.
4. Add to a suggestion made by someone else.

II. List Below Ideas for Solving the Problem

1. _____
2. _____
3. _____
4. _____
5. _____
6. _____
7. _____
8. _____

III. Evaluation Sheet

A. In the spaces below list five
   ideas you have selected
   from your creative thinking
   as worthy of further consideration.

B. Vertically, in the columns
   on the right, write in the
   norms you have chosen.

C. Now go over your list of five
   ideas one by one and judge
   each according to its effectiveness in meeting each
   norm you have chosen on
   an ascending scale of 1 to 4
   (poor to excellent).

D. Next, total the ratings for
   each idea. Then select the
   three with the highest ratings. These are the ideas to
   be used for further consideration in your prayer of
   discernment.

NORMS

Total

1. —————————————————————

2. —————————————————————

3. —————————————————————

4. —————————————————————

5. —————————————————————

*Adapted from the materials used by the Creative Problem Solving Institute
at their summer institutes in Buffalo

PART TWO
NURTURING MATURITY

Chapter X
A Sustaining Life-Style

We all have heard of those who have had a dramatic focal awakening and shortly afterward fallen by the wayside. Some reach out in ministry too far too fast. A mother wrote me some time ago about her teen-age son, whom I had happened to meet in a surly adolescent state of mind and behavior. Three weeks later when I heard from Louise she told me that Bob was in the backyard painting the station wagon red, white, and blue and taking off for an evangelistic tour of the West! He had just received the "Baptism of the Holy Spirit." Quite coincidentally, some time later, I met a clergyman who had had an experience similar to Bob's. It was like the before and after of the same situation. He too had gone immediately into ministry. Now, twenty-five years later, he was in quest of depth; he was experiencing serious spiritual growing pains, and he recognized the need for solitude and prayer in order to sort things out. We need reminding that after his dramatic awakening Paul took off for the desert before launching on an apostolic career. In general, many "turned on" Christians do not have a supportive life-style to sustain them. Inasmuch as we are all creatures of habit, our bad habits must be transformed into good habits. St. Paul speaks of the unspiritual man who does not accept anything of the Spirit of God, he lives in the outer circle on his emotions, senses, and feelings, rather than in the inner circle of his growth center controlled by the Spirit. In other words, good habits need to be formed to enable us to center on Christ within and to have a ruling sense of God's presence.

There are three stages in habit formation which tend to
nurture a mature Christian life. The first stage involves the
removal of sinful obstacles, the next, the removal of those idols
that deter growth, and finally, the formation of those habits that
are a positive help to sustain growth and to nurture the
maturing process. This third stage is considered here; the
formation of habits of solitude, silence, and prayer.

As we mature in our relational faith on the level of expanded
consciousness, we need supportive habits and a sustaining
life-style just as career persons, be they surgeons, musicians,
astronauts, teachers, or executives, need discipline. Good
intentions or a one-time focal awakening are is not enough to
make us pliant in the hands of God and to help us mature in the
fullness of his love from communication to communion in our
growth center. We must be self-controlled and alert to be able
to pray (I Pet. 4:7).

Theresa of Avila says that God gives the gift of communion
with him to those who prepare for it and whose habits enable
them to sustain this life. Many of the difficulties involved, she
claims, are in the beginning. Yet we can never sit back and think
we have it made.

> You must not build upon foundations of prayer and contempla-
> tion alone, for, unless you strive after the virtues and practise
> them, you will never grow to be more than dwarfs. God grant that
> nothing worse than this may happen—for, as you know, anyone
> who fails to go forward begins to go back, and love, I believe, can
> never be content to stay for long where it is.
>
> You may think that I am speaking about beginnings, and that
> later on one may rest: but, as I have already told you, the only
> repose that these souls enjoy is of an interior kind. . . .[1]

We must work at it if we wish to acquire habits to sustain a
mature life-style that will enable us to make our growth center
the central feature of our life. We must constantly strengthen
that inner zone to which we can retire at all times in communion
with the Holy Spirit. To the extent that we do this, he will
deepen our inward relational faith and at the same time we will

mature in our agape love toward others. Our spiritual life will become activated with his power to live and to give.

Solitude

There are certain habits that are especially essential to the nurturing of life in our growth center. Among these are solitude and silence.

Solitude is a necessary condition for maturing from communication to communion. First of all, we must understand its value before we find ourselves willing to make an effort to acquire this habit; therefore, the following insights about solitude may prove helpful.

(1) Solitude is a time when you stop hiding in the group and allow God to fill you with his presence. His word comes to you in solitude and it is in solitude that you make a response.

(2) John of the Cross says, There is no companionship which affords comfort to the soul that longs for God; indeed, until she finds him everything causes greater solitude.[2] In solitude, away from all things, the soul is alone with God as he guides, moves, and raises her to divine things.

(3) Even at its quietest moments, solitude fosters growth from loving communication to intimate communion. Solitude does not mean "absorption" as some wrongly construe the language of the mystics.

(4) Solitude is not the same as loneliness. Rather it is a condition of being alone with love. Solitude opens us to a true creative life and communion with others in God. Loneliness is self-centered, a condition of our sinful state. Solitude, while it does not entirely remove this suffering, gradually opens us to the love that heals and transforms loneliness.

(5) Jesus, forsaken by his friends, said, "Will you also go away?" He suffered isolation because of the mistakes of

others; he was betrayed by one friend, denied by another. Yet he said, "I am not alone for the Father is always with me." His temporary dereliction on the cross, his final suffering in solitude, is a mystery.

(6) Loneliness cannot be overcome by sheer escape from the fact of aloneness. It can be overcome only by being healed and transformed into a relational love, a creative life of solitude in communion, which is proper to the life of the Blessed Trinity.

(7) Solitude and communion are not conflicting elements within our human situation. Each presupposes the other. And as maturing Christians we need to nurture the conditions which will enable us to grow from communication to communion.

(8) A maturing Christian requires periods of solitude and to find these becomes a real responsibility. How can the average person find time to be alone? While some may not find the matter difficult to arrange, there are many who do.

Perhaps there is no greater need of the maturing Christian than to have time each day to be alone. In some cases foresight and planning may be required in order to parcel out even brief periods for solitude. This could mean ruling out trivia or an innocuous TV show which lulls you into a stupor. In *Seeds of Contemplation,* Thomas Merton writes that the love life within our growth center must be draw up like a jewel from the bottom of the sea, rescued from confusion, indistinction, from immersion in the common, the nondescript, the trivial, the sordid. Once we see the value of solitude, we will gradually set aside longer periods of time each week for being alone.

Ideally, Sunday should offer periods of time for solitude and meditation, whether on the beach or in the mountains. It should become for us "God's Workday"; we rest in him as he works in us! "For God has left us the promise that we go in and rest with him. Let us fear that one of you will be found to have failed to go in to that rest" (Heb. 4:10-11).

Silence

Besides solitude, there is a need for habits of silence. It is in silence that we enter our growth center, a sanctuary, an inner haven, the kingdom of God within, where each soul is silent in his presence. It is to this portable temple that we can retreat anytime, anywhere, for cleansing, healing, and unifying as we allow the Father to rest his eyes on us. To enter this sanctuary we must develop outward habits of silence to prepare the way of the Lord, to make straight his path. We must limit our spoken words on occasion to listen to the Word within. Love brings recollection and silence to the soul, it is able to distinguish a voice among thousands of voices, the voice of the Beloved. In solitude it is conscious of a presence who opens the doors of the psyche to an experience of another order, a Christian consciousness which changes the quality of our existence.

We can cultivate a silence reminiscent of those long silent nights Jesus passed on the mountainside during his prayer to God; a silence of Gethesemane and Calvary broken only by a few words. It is this silence in which the soul hears his voice and is conscious of his presence. True communion in silence is the work of the Holy Spirit as we penetrate more deeply into our growth center and find Christ abiding there.

Nurturing maturity, on the level of Christ-consciousness, involves silent, wordless prayer, or simple attention without the imagination. This form of prayer encourages us to develop silence as part of our sustaining life-style. For that reason, it might be important to consider certain aspects of contemplation which nurture silence.

Prayer Habits

We should develop habits of prayer that will enable us to anchor our hearts on the Lord in our growth center, where Christ reigns and where the Holy Spirit instructs. If we do not find our way into the stillness of this center, we cannot hear what the Holy Spirit is saying to us there, and we can therefore be subject to every kind of slavery. All levels of human nature are a risk; the Spirit alone is not a slave.

Our Growth Center

While in solitude and silence we will begin to understand our growth center, that inner sanctuary in which our spiritual life matures in an ever deepening inward relationship with our Lord. Our whole life will take on new meaning as our conscious awareness of this great mystery deepens and our relational faith grows from loving communicaton to intimate communion. This new consciousness of a relational love in our growth center is not a pious notion to be taken lightly. Rather, it is the same root Christianity that is recorded in the New Testament and in spiritual classics throughout the centuries. The following description of our growth center is found in a passage from *The Living Flame* by John of the Cross:

> The soul's Center is God. When it has reached its final and deepest Center in God it will know love and enjoy God with all its might. . . . When it has not reached this point (in its Center) . . . it still has movement and strength for advancing further and is not satisfied. Although it is in its Center, it is not yet in its deepest Center, for it can go deeper in God.[3]

Contemplation

The best definition of contemplation is "rest in him as he works in you." To allow this to happen requires a period of preparation. We first place ourselves in the presence of God by brief reflection on a phrase from our favorite prayer or a passage from scripture. (A selection of appropriate scripture references follows at the end of the chapter.) As we meditate on the sayings of Jesus, there will be leaps of understanding and flashes of contemplative insight which come to us. Usually, reflective meditation on scripture includes listening for the delicate voice of God and a response in colloquy, praise, petition, or resolution. Sometimes it means just listening. "Where thy treasure is, there also will thy heart be" (Matt. 6:21) would be an appropriate scripture, for where your heart is there is your whole being. The secret of recollection and of the presence of God is in the heart; if one is dissipated among many concerns, it is because one's heart has not yet found its treasure.

Once we are in a spirit of loving communication growing into communion, we can shut ourselves off from these reflections and dwell in inner silence and communion with the Holy Spirit within. We can allow ourselves to sink, as it were, downward, downward, into the profound silence and peace that is the essence of the meditative state. We are shutting off the senses and stopping the wheels of the imagination. It is a period of suspension of our reflective powers when we make a deliberate effort to bring our mind to a state of stillness, to stop weaving our own ideas, to reach a point of deep silence and allow the Holy Spirit to speak to our heart.

The Prayer of Silence

John of the Cross, in *Ascent of Mt. Carmel,* observes that at a certain point in time the maturing Christian ought to change his prayer style from one of thinking and reflecting to one that leads him gradually into intimate communion with God. This occurs when the spiritual person simply cannot meditate. John says that the person should now learn to be still in God, fixing his loving attention upon him, in the silence of his understanding. Often then, divine calm and peace will be infused into his soul, together with a wondrously sublime knowledge of God which enfolds the person in divine love. At this point he should not meddle with forms, meditations, and imaginings, *or* any kind of reasoning, lest his soul be disturbed and brought out of its contentment and peace. And if such a person has scruples about doing nothing, let him note that he is doing no small thing by pacifying the soul and bringing it into a divine calm.[4]

John further describes this period as a time of waiting with no desire to feel or see anything. Simone Weil in *Waiting for God* beautifully describes the experience of the maturing Christian waiting for God to reveal himself in the growth center. It is like the servants who are waiting for their master to come home from the marriage feast so that they can open to him at once when he comes and knocks. Blessed are those whom the master finds awake when he comes, for he will have them sit at table and serve them. She writes:

> The servant who will be loved is the one who stands upright and motionless at the door, in a state of vigil, watchfulness, attentiveness and desire, to open as soon as he hears any knocking.
> Nothing will upset his watchful stillness, not to the slightest degree . . . neither tiredness, nor hunger, nor the entreaties, nor friendly invitations, nor injuries.[5]

This is an in-between time in our growth as our prayer life develops from loving communication to intimate communion. It can be a very painful period while we are waiting for God. At one time we alternated between an active vocal prayer and reflective meditation on scripture. Now as we launch into the unknown in wordless prayer, we may become most uncomfortable outside the comfortable home of our thoughts. Yet it is only when we move beyond this point of communication that we begin to mature in a new awareness of God to the highest level of consciousness, communion with God.

Traveling through a desert in the absence of landmarks by which to chart your spiritual route, while surrounded by a never-ending stretch of barren and unfriendly territory, is a trial peculiar to this period of growth and prayer. It reminds us of the way Soren Kierkegaard, in *Fear and Trembling,* speaks of Abraham: "He left one thing—his worldly wisdom, and took on another thing: faith. Otherwise he would have realized the absurdity of his journey and not set out at all."

To wait in silence is anything but slothful egoism. Nothing is more difficult to human nature carried away in action and agitation than to remain in the presence of God under the influence of his purifying love.

It is sometimes difficult to know just when communication ceases and spiritual communion begins. One certain indication is when the initiative comes from God and not from you as he draws your attention within to an awareness of and consciousness of his love and presence.

It is during this period that a maturing process occurs. St. Teresa of Avila has pictured these maturing stages in reference to watering a garden. In the beginning the water is pulled up from the well in a bucket and distributed by hand. Next a contrivance is attached to the well so that the water is pulled up with less labor and emptied into a trough from which a channel takes it to the beds of plants. Then, with no effort to the gardener, other than giving it direction from place to place, a canal supplies the water. Finally, rain descends from heaven requiring no aid from the gardener at all. These are the maturing stages of prayer when your own initiative in wordless prayer is gradually taken over by the Holy Spirit.

Contemplation is not a matter of intelligence or imagination. It takes place on the deepest levels of our growth center where the action of the Holy Spirit meets with only one obstacle, the soul's radical desire to escape God's taking possession of it, a desire which has its roots in rebellion and sin. The more we contemplate, the more we deepen that relationship with the Holy Spirit who will lead us into the mystery of the Trinity, the life of the Three Divine Persons.

A Few Scripture Selections for Reflection

THE CALL TO MATURITY

Eph. 1:3-6	Eph. 4:13	Matt. 5:48
Eph. 4:23-24	Gal. 3:26	2 Cor. 9-10
Eph. 1:13		

GOD'S ABIDING PRESENCE

John 14:16-17, 20, 23   Eph. 3:16-19   2 Cor. 6:16
Gal. 2:20   Heb. 3:6   2 Cor. 13:5
John 18:20

COMMUNION WITH GOD

Heb. 4:1-3, 8-9, 11   John 15:7-8

COMMUNION WITH ANOTHER IN CHRIST

John 17:20, 22   Eph. 2:22   1 Thess. 3:12
John 13:34   1 Thess. 4:9   1 Peter 1:22

AN ACTIVATED FAITH

Eph. 3:20   John 15:16   John 15:7
2 Thess. 3:3   Rom. 12:2   Eph. 3:14-20

A SUSTAINING LIFE-STYLE

Luke 3:4   1 Pet. 4:7

PRAYER FORMS FOR THE MATURING CHRISTIAN

Listening and Guidance   *Forgiveness*
Rom. 12:2   2 Cor. 2:10-11
2 Thess. 3:5   Eph. 4:31-32
John 10:27   Col. 3:13-16
Eph. 5:10

Chapter XI
The Prayer of Referral

Fuel for the Flame

We should be responsive to the privilege of having Christ in us and seek ways to keep in touch with him so that our actions will be permeated with his love and presence. The tragedy is that few avail themselves of this tremendous resource in their growth center. According to God's plan Christ's presence demands a response. If he dwells in our souls together with the Father and the Spirit, we must also live in union with him in the radiance of his love. The continual presence of such a noble guest should not leave us indifferent. For awareness of his presence permits us to be familiar with him in loving communication and to converse in the most intimate manner with the Three Divine Persons at any time, in any place, and in any circumstance. Our response above all else should be marked by a degree of openness and receptivity—like that of Mary—to the workings of the Holy Spirit; we should see ourselves as pilgrim people responding to the breath of the Holy Spirit.

Once we realize the truth that the core of reality is not our ego, nor an inner vacuum, we are on the right path. Once we realize that as we are Christians the redeeming power of the Holy Spirit is at work in our growth center, we are already maturing. Once we are tuned in on sound approaches to prayer that will enable us to integrate our whole life, we are on the way to putting prayer in action. For it is then we begin to realize that no matter what inner struggles or growth hazards arise, we have a place to which we can refer them. Not only that, but personal joys, happy memories, sorrows, and hopes also have a placement center, our growth center.

In the past, we may have felt helpless when faced with the impulses of an unbalanced personality, but now our mature insight tells us that we have a powerhouse within, a place for constant referral in the turmoil of everyday life. In our efforts to integrate the externals of life with life in our growth center, we can make everything fuel for the flame of love. While our efforts at good behavior help to support us, of themselves such efforts can never make us whole. Healing, cleansing, and unifying is the work of the Holy Spirit in our growth center as our psyche is opened to his power through wordless prayer, meditation, and the prayer of referral. There is error, however, in making religon too grim and strenuous an affair. While moral effort must form an integral part of human experience, it is clearly possible to make too much of the process of wrestling with evil. Attention concentrated on the struggle with sins and weaknesses, instead of on the sources of happiness and power, will lead to frustration. Evelyn Underhill points out that the early ascetics who believed in confronting temptations directly got plenty of temptations with which to deal as a result. A sounder method, she claims, is taught in *The Cloud of Unknowing.* When thoughts of sin press on you, it suggests that you look away, look over your shoulder, seek elsewhere, seek God.

Many have the psychological tendency to project their dark side on others. Once again, our growth center is the answer. The reason being that our own ego is simply unable to absorb those evil inclinations that sometimes explode when we go inward. To project one's dark side on a vase, as some meditation groups do, or on another person, a technique used in some human dynamics groups, is not the answer.

Darkness can only be absorbed by light, so we must find something that can absorb our darkness. Simone Weil in *Gateway to God* addressed this very question and came up with a profound understanding. It is only when we project our dark side on something perfectly pure that cannot be defiled, that evil is not reflected back on us.

> A part of the evil that is within us we project onto the objects of our attention and desire; and they reflect it back to us, as if the evil came from them. It is for this reason that any place where we find ourselves submerged in evil inspires us with hatred and disgust. It seems to us that the place itself is imprisoning us in evil. Thus an invalid comes to hate his room and the people around him, even if they are dear to him; and workers sometimes hate their factory, and so on.
>
> But if through attention and love we project a part of our evil upon something perfectly pure, it cannot be defiled by it; it remains pure and does not reflect the evil back on us; and so we are delivered from the evil.[1]

It is in making all in life so much fuel for the flame of love that we begin to experience the healing, purifying, unifying, and deepening of our intimate love of God within our growth center. This can occur in several ways. Simone Weil, for instance, speaks of the healing power of Holy Communion.

> Communion is therefore a journey through fire which burns and destroys a fragment of the soul's impurities. The next communion destroys another fragment. The amount of evil in the human soul is limited, and the divine fire is inexhaustible. Thus, at the conclusion of the operation, in spite of the worst lapses, arrival at the state of perfection cannot fail, provided that there is no betrayal or deliberate refusal of the good, and that the accident of death does not intervene.[2]

Another approach is through spiritual communion: the prayer of referral, whereby all in life can become so much fuel for the flame of love in your growth center. Moreover, receiving Holy Communion can be all the more unifying, purifying, and healing if we prepare ourselves through the consistent use of the prayer of referral.

As maturing Christians we can learn to integrate our lives around communion with God in our growth center through the prayer of referral which in some respects resembles the Jesus Prayer. Everything in life can become fuel for the flame of love. Brother Lawrence says:

> He requires no great matters of us in a little adoration from time to time; sometimes to pray for His grace; sometimes to return Him thanks for the favors He has given you and still gives you in the midst of your troubles and to console yourself with Him. Lift up your heart to Him. You need not cry very loud; He is nearer to us than we are aware.[3]

The approach described here offers a norm from which to deviate, since it can be adapted to meet individual needs. Moreover, it provides a prayer form supportive of the maturing life in your growth center, prayer in action, by fostering a ruling sense of God's presence.

The maturing of our relational faith in our growth center is in itself the work of the Holy Spirit whose activity increases as we desire him and yield to his quiet action. Paul writes in 2 Thessalonians 1:11, "May he fulfill by his power all your desire for goodness and complete your work of faith." The soul hardly perceives the moments of this mysterious action, and only after long stretches of experience can it realize the changes which the Holy Spirit has worked.

The Prayer of Referral

The prayer of referral is the simple referring of all in life to your growth center in which dwells the Holy Spirit. The habit of prayer needs to be formed to enable us to make everything in life fuel for the flame of love. At an immature stage of life, when we lived on the surface, such a thing might not have occurred to us. But as we mature, the deeper we go into our growth center the greater the need becomes for mature habits of prayer to deal with our life problems, to offer love and praise—on this new level of consciousness.

The Prayer of Referral

There are four aspects to this prayer approach:
1. Reflection
2. Projection
3. The prayer-carrier
4. The goal

Reflection: relates to prayerful use of a suitable scripture passage in line with our need or disposition.

Projection: pertains to the object we want to refer—the fuel—be it worry, anxiety or some hope, desire, gratitude.

The Prayer-
   Carrier: the prayer or "breather" that we use when we refer all to the living flame, e.g., the Jesus Prayer, the Doxology

The Goal: is the growth center, that inner realm where dwells the Holy Spirit—the love of the Father and the Son—the living flame

How to Use the Prayer of Referral

Reflect on a phrase from scripture in line with your particular need or disposition. Then, select a short prayer as a prayer-carrier, such as the Doxology, which bears with it the power of Christ and his church throughout the ages, a prayer that scatters the powers of darkness and brightens our lives with holiness. "Glory be to the Father, and to the Son, and to the Holy Spirit; as it was in the beginning, is now and ever shall be, world without end. Amen."

Reflection	*Projection*	*Prayer-Carrier*
Lamb of God who takes away the sins of the world have mercy on us. (John 1:29)	Concern for evil in the world. Your own disorderly inclinations. The injustices—violence, crime	The Doxology or the Jesus Prayer

Don't worry about anything. Instead pray about everything. Tell God your needs; and don't forget to thank him. (Phil. 4:4-7)	Anxiety Worry about anything Personal concerns	

I would like you to be free from worry. (1 Cor. 7:32) Cast all your concern on him. (1 Pet.) Worry is of Satan.		

And God our source of peace will soon crush Satan under your feet. (Rom. 16:20)	Tension Excitement Agitation Irritation Confusion	

Peace is of God and will conquer Satan.	

My peace be with you. (Luke 24:36)	

You will have peace through your union with me. (John 16:33)	Addictions Hangups Egocentrism Religious egoism

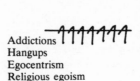

He will give complete freedom to those who are his. (Eph. 1:14)

Keep your roots deep in him. (Col. 2:7)

Abide in me. (John 15:4)

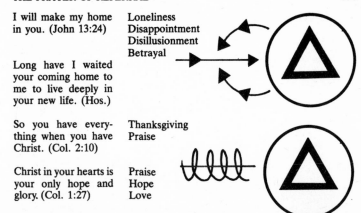

I will make my home in you. (John 13:24)	Loneliness Disappointment Disillusionment Betrayal
Long have I waited your coming home to me to live deeply in your new life. (Hos.)	
So you have everything when you have Christ. (Col. 2:10)	Thanksgiving Praise
Christ in your hearts is your only hope and glory. (Col. 1:27)	Praise Hope Love

You may be asking: "How do I know that the prayer of referral is for me?" One simple way to decide is to ask yourself whether it has meaning for you at this point in your spiritual life? Spiritual writers say that when you read a spiritual book, you should take from it only what feeds your own spirit and let the rest go. The same principle applies here. If the prayer of referral meets a need in your life, begin to use it. It is not a prayer form for beginners, who are inclined to grab for gimmicks, but rather for the maturing Christian who had a focal awakening and is developing a supportive life-style and a deep relational faith in the growth center. It is meant for those who are growing from communication to communion and are struggling to integrate their prayer life with their actions. It is meant for those who recognize that everything in life can become a means—not an idol—of grace—a sacramental— fuel for the flame of love within the growth center.

At this point we are reminded of those words of Catherine of Siena which clearly describe the role of the Holy Spirit within:

What more couldst Thou give me than Thyself? Thou art the fire which ever burns, without being consumed; Thou consumest in Thy heat all the soul's self-love; Thou art the fire which takes away all cold; with Thy light Thou doest illuminate me so that I may know all Thy truth.[4]

It is important to develop habits of prayer to replace our immature ones of former days if we want to "renew our hearts and the face of the earth." Chardin, in substance, speaks of the prayer of referral when he observes:

Whoever is conscious of the presence at the center of his being, of the very active stream of God's truth and love, is impelled to turn back to it again and again to purify, renew, tranquilize himself there. He knows that he can shoulder the responsibility for the world without danger . . . only so long as he is inwardly in relation to his God. . . . a child . . . unreservedly . . . open.[5]

Christ is still seeking you. He is offering himself to you at every moment, in every place. When you realize this everything becomes bread to feed you, fire to purify you, and a chisel to shape you according to his image. Everything becomes a means of grace, fuel for the flame of love. Now you begin to see that the One you used to seek in specific ways is himself seeking you incessantly and giving himself to you in *everything* that happens.

St. Gregory speaks of the experience of the divine presence in your growth center as a living fire, the Holy Spirit. He is not just the guest of your soul; he is love, and love is never idle. He is the living fire which never ceases to consume, inflame, and diffuse the life of God into your soul. Scripture says "The Spirit has given us life; he must also control our lives" (Gal. 5:25). Whether you eat or drink, or whatever you do, do all for the glory of God.

Once you have an awareness of God's presence, the next step is to integrate life in your growth center around this central focus by forming sustaining prayer habits.

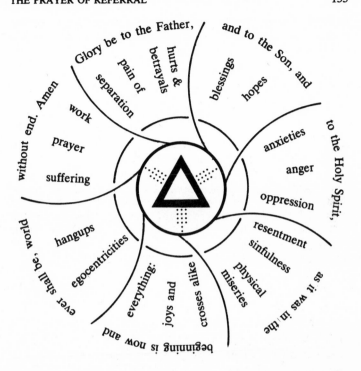

There is no fuel for the flame of love like the wood of the cross.
Elizabeth of the Trinity

As our spiritual life matures, we are gradually able to integrate the whole of life around communion in our growth center and to find unity and purpose as the love within keeps on growing more and more (Phil. 1:9). We begin to feel Christ's presence and power at work in our growth center (Eph. 1:19). Now each event in life becomes so much fuel for the flame of love, enabling us to grow into the fullness of his love. We can be certain that the action of that over-ruling love will not fail. Often it is we who resist and become bewildered, because we are not yielding ourselves to the steady guiding power of the Holy Spirit and are forgetting the real source of

our life. Regret for errors past and anxiety about the future
keep us bound. As we mature, there comes a gradual
realization that each event is directly linked to the quiet action
of God. Through all the vicissitudes of trial, sin, and conflict,
the ground of our soul is rooted in his life and love.

Because of his presence in our growth center, everything in
life not only takes on new meaning, but becomes a means of
growth, a means of reaching maturity, a means of giving him
glory!

Chapter XII
A New Look at the Jesus Prayer

This prayer should appeal to all maturing Christians, particularly those who have been exposed to oriental meditation, to Transcendental Meditation (T.M.) and its mantras, the inner vibrations of which are meant to raise the level of consciousness. For those who would like to practice meditation in the context of Christianity, there is no better way than through the Jesus Prayer. It is a prayer which can be used by all those interested in nurturing life in their growth center and for whom this prayer holds an appeal.

The Jesus Prayer is also for those who would like a form, but want their prayer life to be more than form. For as you will see after a while the form vanishes as this prayer becomes a way of life. The Jesus Prayer is for those who would like to blend a life of prayer with a life of action, for those who would like "to pray without ceasing" effortlessly. It is for those who are biblical in their orientation and may hold suspect any form of prayer not based on Scripture. No sounder scriptural prayer can be found than the use of the name of Jesus.

Probing Your Spiritual Roots

The Jesus Prayer is one of the most profound prayers in the history of Christianity, dating back to apostolic times. The original writings from the Greek Fathers of the church about this prayer are to be found in five volumes preserved in the monasteries of Mt. Athos in Greece. There is a shorter version in English called *The Philokalia*. Some persons enjoy reading *The Way of the Pilgrim,* an allegory which gives an account of a pilgrim seeking to learn the meaning of Paul's words "pray without ceasing." Eventually the pilgrim finds a monk who teaches him the Jesus Prayer. Since early Christian times, a way of life founded on the Jesus Prayer prevailed in Eastern monasteries; it was known as Hesychasm.

As Happhold points out, the Jesus Prayer is a form of meditation. He says that although the practice of meditation has always been present in Christianity, the objectives at different periods have not always been the same. Nor has the same weight been given to meditation in Western Christianity as is given to it in Hinduism and Buddhism.

In Hinduism and Buddhism, and indeed among the Sufis of Islam, the chief object of the spiritual exercise of meditation is the deliberate raising and enlargement of consciousness for the purpose of enlightenment. In Christianity, on the other hand, there has been a tendency, particularly since the sixteenth century, to judge the value of meditation in terms of growth in virtue. Spiritual directors and writers on meditation frowned on any spiritual exercise whose goal was to produce a mystical state of mind or which deliberately enabled the meditator to move into a state of contemplation. If God leads you into such a state well and good. But this state must not be sought or expected.

This particular bias, however, has not been characteristic of all periods of Christian history. Nor is it universal. For instance, Eastern theologians and spiritual directors of the early Christian church considered the objective of spiritual exercises to be "illumination" and "deification." They believed that by means of spiritual exercises these states could be reached. We can view the goal of the Jesus Prayer in this light also.

Besides these objectives, the Jesus Prayer, the Prayer of the Heart, typical of the deepest meditational practices of the Eastern Orthodox Church, has as its goal that enlargement and elevation of spiritual consciousness which is characteristic of Hindu and Buddhist meditation.

The Jesus Prayer as a Mantra

Although the mantra is extensively used and occupies an important place in the spiritual exercises of Hinduism and Buddhism and is practiced in the Eastern Orthodox Church in the Prayer of Jesus, it has not been emphasized in the spiritual exercises of the Western church. That is not to say that mantras have not been used, but only that they have not been generally understood as a prayer form. For instance, take our use of the Greek, "Kyrie Eleison, Christe Eleison, Kyrie Eleison: Lord have mercy, Christ have mercy, Lord have mercy," used for centuries in the eucharistic celebration or the rosary recited by Roman Catholics. The mantra is recommended as an aid to contemplation in that ancient medieval classic, *The Cloud of Unknowing*. So what is a mantra?

(1) It is a word, a phrase, or a sentence which keeps your mind from wandering and encourages recollection.
(2) It is a prayer form, a microcosm of an eternal reality, which you may wish to contemplate; or it it is used to awaken dormant forces in your soul, to establish contact with your depth consciousness, or as a means of doing what Paul advises, stir up the Spirit within.
(3) It is also an auditory stimulus, the repetition of which awakens the latent consciousness as music does.[1]

How to Practice the Jesus Prayer

The Jesus Prayer is suited to the beginner as well as the most mature Christian. It is adaptable to every phase of the maturing process as you grow in your relational faith from communication to communion.

1. It begins with the continual repetition of the name of Jesus aloud, in a place where you can be alone. Repeating the prayer aloud is regarded as a means of acquiring the habit and of conditioning the body.

2. The Jesus Prayer is then repeated silently, slowly, and deliberately all during the day. Silent repetition is a means of acquiring concentration. At this stage the prayer becomes reflective.

3. Next the Jesus Prayer is accommodated to the breathing processes of inhaling and exhaling by rhythmically breathing the name of Jesus.

4. When the habit of concentration has been acquired, it is then possible to take the prayer down into the heart where it lives of itself, with every breath and heartbeat.

5. At this final stage, the saying of the prayer to the beats of the heart is first visualized and then listened to as the words are breathed. The blending of your breathing and heartbeat can bring about a unity of being which will have a transforming effect on your whole life.

6. Eventually, the prayer will repeat itself, and the mind will be half-conscious of it going on even while you are busy with many things. This prayer begins in solitude and silence but can later be taken into the marketplace when it begins to live with every heartbeat.

The Way of the Pilgrim leads to this very point. As indicated earlier, the pilgrim fails to understand how this might be done until he meets a monk who teaches him the Jesus Prayer.

As described above, the Jesus Prayer effects a union of mind and heart. It is a prayer that moves us from the head center to the heart center of being. What was first understood intellectually is now understood intuitively, and so the prayer of Jesus becomes an instrument in the transformation of the whole being. Jesus' name can bring the soul into unity because the word carries with it the power of Christ and the Holy Spirit. ("Jesus" is not a meaningless mantra!)

A monk of the Orthodox Church suggests that in using the name of Jesus, the approach should be gentle, easy, and graceful as a bird that sails in the sky, beating its wings only from time to time. You should rest in the Lord and resume the Jesus mantra when thoughts threaten. He warns that not everyone should use this prayer form, but only those attracted to it under the guidance of the Holy Spirit, and only if it produces an increase of love and peace. The Jesus Prayer can take many forms; what is important is that the name of Jesus be the center of the prayer. In the East, the most common form is, "Lord Jesus, Son of God, have mercy upon me a sinner." The simple use of the name of Jesus alone, however, is the most ancient form.

Happhold observes that in the Epistle of St. Paul to the Galatians you find a perfect Christian mantra: "I am crucified with Christ. Nevertheless I still live but it is not I any more; it is Christ who now lives in me" (2:20). This can be called the "transformation-into-Christ" mantra, the transformation of the physical man into the spiritual man. Actually, it is two mantras which may be used combined or separately. This mantra is the epitome of the spiritual growth process; the first part is the renouncement of the lower self, "I am crucified with Christ." The second part expresses the transformation which results from the renouncements and the inner realization of a relationship with the Christ who dwells within. In practice, when said in Greek, this mantra may be reduced to seven words: *Christo sunestauromai. Ouketi ego. Christos en emoi.* Those who do not care to use the Greek can make use of this mantra in English, Christ in me and I in Him.[2]

Happhold claims that the theory held by those involved in T.M., that mantras without meaning can be valuable, may hold some truth. Particular sounds have a psychological effect on the human psyche just as music sometimes strikes deep chords of feelings. For Westerners, it may be necessary for a mantra to be more than a sound to have its full effect. Taking this one step further, not only is it good to have a meaning, but even better to have a mantra which is a means of grace. The Jesus Prayer besides being a mantra with meaning is a means of grace, a sacramental. When you use a mantra such as the Jesus Prayer, so pregnant with power as well as meaning, you can only agree that the use of a meaningless mantra is immature.

Nurturing Maturity Through the Jesus Prayer

The Jesus Prayer can be used at all stages of the spiritual growth process from communication to communion. When you identify with Jesus in your growth center, through the use of his name, you are nurturing your inward relational faith. The use of the name of Jesus has a purifying effect on your spirit and penetrates you like a drop of oil penetrates a cloth. It becomes a source of strength to paralyze the forces of evil and to overcome the law of sin (Rom. 7:23).

The use of the name of Jesus can bring about a focal awakening to the reality of his presence in your growth center. As you reverently worship Jesus (Matt. 2:11), the use of his name is a means of healing and forgiveness. It is a filter through which your thoughts, words, and deeds pass and are freed from impurities.

We pronounce the name of Jesus so that he may more fully dwell in our hearts (Eph. 3:17). As we meditate the inner reality of his name will pass into the depths of our growth center, and we will more fully realize that growing in loving communication to intimate communion is our call as Christians.

In this special way we begin to put on the Lord Jesus Christ (Rom. 13:14). It is the living content of the name of Jesus which enters into us physically, like an ointment poured forth over the body (Song of Songs 1:3).

The Jesus Prayer integrates the whole of our life around the central reality of God's love and presence. It simplifies and unifies our maturing spiritual life because the power of the Word is there to do it. The divided personality which said "my name is legion" will recover wholeness in the sacred name: "unite my heart to fear thy name" (Ps. 86:11 KJV).

While growing in our relational faith the Jesus Prayer will have increasing significance as a form of spiritual communion and an "inner eucharist." It is an inner but very real approach to our Lord, distinct from an approach to his person as food; it is a partaking of this food invisibly. This spiritual communion becomes easier when it is given expression in the name of Jesus. We can pronounce the name with the intention of feeding our souls on the Sacred Body and Blood that we approach through the name of Jesus. Such a communion can be renewed as often as we like. In this name we are united with all who share the eucharistic meal. Its use is also a preparation for receiving Jesus in the Eucharist.

These reflections on the Jesus Prayer bring to mind the relationship of Jesus to the Trinity. Jesus was conceived in Mary of the Holy Spirit. He remained through his whole earthly life the receiver of the gift of the Holy Spirit. He was led by the Spirit into the desert (Matt. 4:1). "The Spirit of the Lord is upon me."

In pronouncing the name of Jesus we can make ourselves one with him in our surrender to the Spirit. We can see Jesus as he breathes the Spirit on the apostles. It was only after the coming of the Holy Spirit at Pentecost that the apostles announced the name with power. In concluding these comments about the Jesus Prayer and the relationship of Jesus to the Trinity, let us note that Jesus is the living Word uttered by the Father. Jesus said "Believest thou not that I am in the Father and the Father in me?"

For those preparing for a prayer ministry certain points should be understood about the Jesus Prayer.

1. The Jesus Prayer should not be considered the ideal prayer form to the exclusion of other prayers such as, reflective meditation or contemplation and wordless prayer, for it is perfectly compatible with all other forms of prayer and can be used to supplement them.
2. The Jesus Prayer is significant in prayer ministry. Reciting the holy name of Jesus is a powerful means of releasing Jesus

in others where he may be imprisoned. It is a means of collaborating with him as he transfigures them into his very likeness. "In my name they shall cast out devils, lay hands on the sick and they shall recover" (Matt. 7:22).

3. There are numerous opportunities to encourage reverence for the name of Jesus and to foster its use among maturing Christians. For example, you can make the most of its misuse by many well-intentioned Christians who use the name of Jesus in vain in crisis situations. It would be unfortunate to discourage its use at such times when in fact Jesus is really needed! Instead, simply stress a change in tone, a reverent use of the name of Jesus in critical situations explaining that this can draw down blessings, strength, comfort, and peace.

4. It is timely to encourage the Jesus Prayer among those already familiar with the use ot T.M. mantras. They already have a headstart on which to build. Using the Jesus Prayer as a mantra will make a person, in one fell swoop, a Christian meditator.

Chapter XIII
A Prayer of Forgiveness and Blessing

Nurturing maturity at the level of Christ-consciousness requires considerable attention to our growth center. From birth—some say before birth—no human being escapes being hurt by others. It may not always be intentional, but it happens regularly. Some who feel themselves singular targets of injustice are labeled paranoid; whereas they may be simply gifted with keen perception! As the saying goes, if we think someone is out to get us, we are not necessarily paranoid; we are probably right.

It often seems that those who label others do so in self-defense, because they are themselves offenders. While we may all be paranoid at times, this does not change the general situation nor our continued vulnerability. The solution to this problem lies at the very heart of Christianity itself. We are told to ask God to bless those who persecute us (Rom. 12:4), yet doing this is another story. Christians, while often ingenious and creative in their ways of spreading the gospel message, seem less resourceful and concerned with applying that message to their own personal situation.

The personal wrongs we are called to forgive differ for each of us and often call for heroism. For instance, you may be chairman of the board one day and find yourself manipulated out of a job the next year. You may be an executive secretary for a lifetime and then find yourself eased out of full benefits by an early retirement. Or you may be one of those creative persons who has just completed all the legwork on an original project when your competitor moves in and takes over everything. Maybe you have been faded into oblivion by the military. Perhaps your spouse has let you down, or your unreasonable adolescent has taken off in a huff. As a young adult you may be disillusioned with the erratic performance of alcoholic parents. Maybe you are a crippled Vietnam veteran, your life ruined by a war in which you never believed. You complete the list.

Of course most of us are aware of Christ's command to forgive our enemies, and we do make a noble effort at times. There is always the pasty smile and handshake. It is fine performance and good window-dressing. But the gaping wounds still need healing. Some say time will do it. Others say, "Just explode, let what's inside out." No one these days would dare suggest repression. Often, even going through the motions of forgiving on the conscious level is heroic and will certainly draw down God's blessing, but it is still immature Christianity. In regard to this William Johnston writes:

> One may succeed in forgiving in the conscious mind (and this is enough for salvation) but the unconscious lags behind, leaving our love so much less human. But through meditation a deeper level of awareness is opened up. Love and faith, if only they are present, can now seep down into the more profound caverns of consciousness and into the subtler layers.[1]

Actually it is love at your growth center which needs to be activated. For the love of the Holy Spirit alone can heal your wounds, your strength renew. Beyond all conscious thinking about how right we really were and how unjustly we were treated, we need to use the prayer of referral making all fuel for the flame of love. Johnston observes:

> And one is liberated only by continuing to love. By fixing one's heart on the cloud of unknowing with deep peace, one becomes detached from turbulent uprisings; and then they wither and die, leaving only love. It is by loving at the ultimate point, by going beyond all categories to the deepest centre, that one is liberated from jealousy

and hatred and the rest. But this is an agonizing purification. All this is particularly evident in that form of love which we call forgiveness. Most psychologists will agree that one of the most damaging traumas that can exist in the memory is suppressed anger and refusal to forgive.[2]

Only love can heal, a love from the source where the healing of one's depths occurs and lasting forgiveness is realized. Christ may command us to forgive our enemies, but he alone can give us the power, and this power comes from our growth center. The question might well be raised, How did our Lord show us what to do? He forgave his executioners. "Father, forgive them, they don't know what they do."

And this is true. He could not deny the crime. He excused the motive. Ignorance. They didn't know what they were doing. The Pharisees were blinded by pride. The executioners no doubt were drunk. He alone knew the actuality of the suffering inflicted in every nerve and sinew of his torn body. We have to experience a particular suffering to know what it is like. Few know the suffering they inflict since it is a suffering they have not experienced. Some years ago, in *Black Like Me,* Howard Griffin recounted his personal experiences disguised as a black man in the South. It was only then that he realized in his own psyche the hurts black persons had been suffering. Maybe this can be said to some degree of those who hurt us—"They don't know what they are doing to me." At this point we are reminded of those words of scripture: "Ask God to bless those who persecute you" (Rom. 12:14). And again in 1 Peter 3:9 "Do not pay back with evil . . . pay back with a blessing."

At best, this is not a natural procedure for beginners, for those who have not had a focal awakening nor experienced a relational faith. The usual reaction is to flee rather than do anything positive or concrete about the matter. The prayer of forgiveness and blessing, another aspect of the prayer of referral, does something positive, something concrete. This form of prayer is "love on the offensive." "Do not let evil defeat you; instead, conquer evil with good" (Rom. 12:21). It is a counterattack from your growth center which puts love into action.

To bless means that we bombard our offender with prayer and put him under God's influence. This immediately relieves us of the self-imposed responsibility for his reform—in some cases a huge relief! We no longer have to rethink the whole traumatic experience; we simply take the spiritual offensive.

When we bless, we break negative thought waves by bringing the Holy Spirit, the living Christ within us, between us and the offender. From a purely psychological point of view this is important. For today, we know from psychology how intensive thought patterns can affect another person for better or worse. Directing your negative thoughts through a blessing of Christ converts the negative into the positive. Our hurt becomes so much fuel for the flame within our growth center. The amount of fuel may even later effect the intensity of the blessing received by both us and the offender. This is not merely pious talk. It can happen and does happen and should happen, since this is what Christianity is all about. The highest form of agape love is forgiveness of enemies from the heart. The heart, over which the Holy Spirit reigns supreme, can alone heal all wounds.

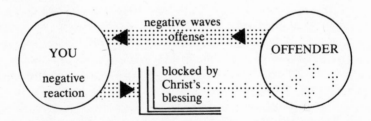

A point worth remembering is that in God's plan, we may well have the responsibility of becoming channels of grace and salvation—through forgiveness—for the very ones who have injured us. There are instances in scripture which suggest this. Picture Stephen being stoned, asking, with hands uplifted, that this crime "be not laid to their charge" as Paul stood by seething with hatred and consenting to Stephen's death. The fact that Paul makes a special note of this incident points to a relationship between Stephen's prayer for forgiveness at the time of his martyrdom and Paul's dramatic conversion.

In this regard we are reminded of what Evelyn Underhill has to say:

Forgiveness
There is nothing more purifying, more redeeming than the love which is awakened by the generous forgiveness of another love. It opens a door in the brick wall which self-esteem has built between itself and God.[3]

The social injuries which are inflicted on many today require a special kind of healing and blessing for those offenders who represent a manipulative culture. Our century, which has had wide experience of how evil man can be, seems to be getting used to the monstrous and to give odd prestige to the pathological and the disgraceful. For those who are on the cutting edge, for those who seek social renewal, an intense reaction to maltreatment, mishandling of reputation, and the like, could produce hatred, resentment, and even rage, without some prayerful intervention. These are the offended who need most to pray for their enemies, if they hope to mature.

Can you imagine what could happen if whole segments of our society, in communion with the Holy Spirit in their growth centers, were to concentrate their prayer and love power one by one on the world malefactors? Fortunately, love can destroy evil, and Christians are protected by the blood of the Lamb and by one who can kill Satan with his breath! (Thess. 2:8).

One other obvious point should be noted here. Christians also inflict injuries inadvertently, thoughtlessly, and selfishly. Sometimes efforts to repair damage actually make matters worse, like rubbing salt in wounds. In some complicated situations apologies and gestures of reconciliation seem meaningless to the injured one. In such cases another dimension of this same prayer of blessing can be used. In fact this may be the only way to meet our obligation not to let the sun go down on our anger. Neglect will never do; this may be the only way open to us to proceed.

The same general procedure shown above in the prayer of blessing can be adapted. As we refer our own offenses against another person to Christ for forgiveness, we request a loving blessing on the one we have offended.

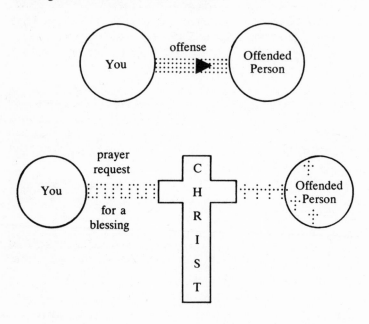

It is worth our effort to acquire the habit of using the prayer of blessing as part of a sustaining life-style, because we will need to use it many times before we die! Review the following steps so that when the next minor or major offense occurs action can be taken at once. In the beginning, we may need to take time out, in solitude and silence. As we grow this practice will become part of our life to be used quietly anytime, anywhere.

On the First Occasions

1. Relax and commune with the Holy Spirit in your growth center. Invoke the name of Jesus.
2. Expose your hurt and negative thoughts to the healing power of the spirit of Jesus.
3. Imagine the person before you as you ask Jesus to bless him or her with his healing love.
4. Ask God to dispel all the powers of darkness as you recite: "Glory be to the Father and to the Son and to the Holy Spirit, as in the beginning, so now, and evermore."

An Evening Prayer

1. Each night before retiring offer a prayer of praise and thanksgiving to God. Thank him for the blessings of the day.
2. Then briefly recall those who in some way have hurt you during the day. Refer them to Christ in your growth center and ask him to bless them.
3. Recall also those you have offended. Ask Jesus to bless them. Promise to repair the mistake in a simple way when the occasion arises.
4. Go to sleep in the Lord.
5. Wake up having grown deeper in your inward relational faith and in a relational faith toward others in agape love.

PART THREE
FOSTERING MATURITY

Chapter XIV
Maturing for Ministry

Are those who experience a Christian consciousness empowered for a special ministry? This puzzled me at the time of the newly emerging neo-Pentecostal movement, when Christians I knew who experienced an awareness of the presence of God in meditation showed no signs of a healing ministry, while others had gifts of ministry such as discernment and did not reflect a prayer gift. I asked Walter Hollenweger, a world-renowned Pentecostal authority, about this. He called my attention to the English theologian Simon Tugwell who had recently published a book entitled *Have You Received the Spirit?*

Tugwell points out that whether in contemplation or in miracles it is the same Spirit of God expressing himself in and through us in various ways. Christ is not divided. Our life in him is fundamentally Christ himself living his own life in us. There is only one reality—which is the mystery of Christ—whether this reality expresses itself in the transformation of our lives through wisdom, contemplative prayer, or the working of miracles, it is all the same Spirit . . . the same Lord working all in all. The mysterious reality of the life of Christ in us should challenge those who are simply content to be baptized and do not aspire to a supernatural awareness of him or to a witness with him in the power of the Spirit.

It is the same Holy Spirit expressing himself in us in ways which enhance our natural gifts just as he did in the disciples and apostles on Pentecost. We come more alive where we are.

152

For instance, if we are teachers, counselors, administrators, or artists—whatever our natural talents might be—they are enhanced, and often those that are dormant come alive. Tugwell says we should not make too sharp a distinction between sanctification and mission; both have their source in a common love life given us by Christ in the Holy Spirit.

Moreover, charismatic works are "paranormal." As Tugwell points out, they are natural psychic phenomena inspired by the Holy Spirit of God. The same principle mentioned in relation to the distinction between religious consciousness and Christian consciousness applies here too. What makes our works Christian is that they are integrated into the mystery of Christ. What makes them Christian is their context and significance. As a matter of fact, as soon as we open up the psychic field we can go in any number of directions, natural, supernatural, or occult.[1] That is why it is so important to be first centered in Christ.

Christian consciousness, as it relates to Christian maturity, can also be viewed in terms of maturity for ministry. Based on observation I came to a few conclusions about this, and once more I asked myself, What is the main focus? Is it success? Personal acclaim, egocentrism? Wealth? Miracles? Or is the core reality of God's love and presence the essence?

I began to realize, as I reflected further, that the world is pleased by a materially successful Christian, because in our achievement-oriented culture we are inclined to say that the test of something good is that it works. I believe success as a goal is quite laudable, but not as a primary goal.

There is still another way of looking at success as it relates to ministry. Not in terms of material advantages or results in ministry, but rather in terms of the happiness of knowing that he is with us supporting us all the way and is the source of our strength. "For we are not to rejoice that the spirits are subject to us . . . but that our names are written in heaven" (Luke 10:20). That heaven brings with it the peace and love of the kingdom of Christ, enriching us for ministry.

So when a ministry, in the dimension of Christian consciousness, has as its first aim success in bringing others to a deeper love of Christ, and when those involved are growing in relational love, the approach is mature. What in fact places such a ministry in a mature category is the *personal* love of Christ inherent in it. This is the determinant factor; this is the clue to what things really mean. The main focus is that love vitality which accompanies the healing power of the Holy Spirit, a love which transcends time, and when channelled through prayer will carry over into eternity. A deep love and peace which can be transmitted to others in a mature ministry of inner healing, of which physical healing in Christian mystery is merely symbolic.

Success then, in terms of maturity for ministry, holds little importance save in relation to the love of Christ and a sharing of that love with others. Tugwell points out that there are "wonder-workers" who reflect no love. It is love that makes our "miracles" acceptable, a love that is not self-seeking, jealous, vain, or conceited, but delights in the truth. I remember the film *The Gospel According to Matthew* of some years ago in which Jesus was represented as a wonder-worker par excellence. Upon leaving the theatre I asked my Protestant friend, "What do you think?" Her response, "There were miracles, but no love."

Instruction

Fostering maturity includes instruction, counseling, and prayer ministry. It means returning to our roots and the great spiritual classics in order to understand the nature of spiritual maturity and the growth process. We begin with ourselves, and there is no better way to do this than through spiritual reading in order to fill in the gaps in our own background. Using books as spiritual guides, we can select reading which meets our specific needs along the road to maturity.

A form of instruction found to be appropriate, appealing, and workable for a wide variety of people of different ages and backgrounds is "reading conversations." A well-informed person or a spiritual counselor can be the coordinator for an entire group in working out reading plans suited to the needs and aspirations of various smaller groups of "reading partners." Or, individuals may strike out on their own with a reading partner of their choice, and the steps that follow may be useful to them also.

Decide upon a reading agenda, a regular time to meet to discuss one or several chapters of the reading material agreed upon. *Prayer in Action* has been written to be instructional as well as inspirational, so my suggestion is that you begin with it. The opening chapters describe the meaning of maturity as related to Christian consciousness, a suitable life-style to support this new way of life, and mature prayer forms. It is likely that after discussing the material in this book, you will want to work out a prayer program using some of the prayer forms suggested such as the prayer of referral, the prayer of blessing, the Jesus Prayer, and the prayer of listening.

Counseling for Maturity

As noted above, a way to foster maturity is through spiritual counseling. This is a ministry to the growing Christian in need of *occasional* guidance, support, and encouragement while maturing in a relational and activated faith experience. If we probe our roots we learn that the early Christians also stressed the need for spiritual counseling. In fact, all great religions have insisted on the necessity of a spiritual guide when we first open up a new dimension of consciousness to avoid falling into pits of non-productive effort while learning and maturing. Consultation with a knowledgeable person is considered vitally important.

According to Thomas Merton, Evelyn Underhill, and others, spiritual counseling is not the same as psychological counseling or psychoanalysis. These are concerned primarily with personality changes. Spiritual counseling focuses on our life

with God leading to a transformation in our deepest psyche
through the power of the Holy Spirit, a depth to which
psychoanalysis cannot penetrate.

Counseling for maturity can mean any number of things.
Here, it is considered an important aspect of the ministry for
maturity because it guides those who are striving for maturity in
finding ways to

a) remove obstacles to growth, such as idols and resentments
   and a lack of forgiveness; and

b) learn to listen with increasing sensitivity to the Holy
   Spirit.

Those involved in this ministry have no other model than
Jesus Christ himself, who for three and a half years in
fulfillment of Isaiah's prophecy (9:6, 11:12) was the Counselor
who guided, instructed, encouraged, and taught his disciples.
Upon his leave-taking, he calmed their anxieties by telling them
he would send them another Counselor—the Holy Spirit—to
be with them to teach and guide them (John 14:26). The Holy
Spirit is not only the guide, but the source of our maturity.

It is not uncommon for spiritual counseling to be done by
Christians who know each other in the Lord and who
themselves are sufficiently informed and mature to be helpful to
each other. There is a need, however, for each church to
assume the responsibility for fostering maturity through an
established form of ministry, call it what you will. The time has
come when counseling must go beyond putting fires out and
dealing with crises. It should also be directed to our common
responsibility as Christians to foster maturity as the call of all.

Counseling should only be offered on a time to time basis
when a particular need arises, to discourage over-dependency.
While it should be done by an informed person, the primary
requisite is that the counselor have a deep inward-toward
relational faith. Among other things, a spiritual counselor can
enable us to discover a supportive life-style and prayer life
congenial with our stage of spiritual growth. A counselor can
enable us to recognize the choices which we need to make so

that the life in our growth center will flourish. A spiritual counselor keeps before us a choice of tasks that are most conducive to a maturing life in our growth center. At the same time, a spiritual counselor will enable us to recognize that uncongenial and unavoidable aspects of life—tasks, human relations, whatever—can become sources of spiritual power when used as so much fuel for the flame of love.

In preparing to foster maturity through counseling, the counselor learns to listen to the Holy Spirit and is thus better able to encourage us to do the same in our personal and social decisions. In general, a successful search for direction will depend upon our sensitivity to the Holy Spirit and our ability to listen to him who speaks to us within our growth center. In communion with him, either in the Eucharist or in prayer, we discover the unique meaning of our lives and how to respond to his maturing love.

Revelation 2:17 speaks of a white stone on which is inscribed a new name that no one knows except the person who receives it and the Lord who gives it. This is symbolic of the unique spiritual direction which ultimately comes to each of us from the indwelling God deep within our growth center.

Counseling with Prayer Ministry

Counseling should always be accompanied by prayer: frequently the prayer for spiritual and inner healing which has a direct bearing on the spiritual growth process.

Spiritual healing is usually concerned with bondages resulting from anger, resentment, anxiety, or blocks due to unjust hurts which only the Spirit of God can heal. As already noted, wounds cannot be healed by a surface act of forgiveness. Prayer of a special kind is needed since anger and resentment prevent the inflow of God's love and peace. The prayer of blessing is one such prayer. While it can be used alone, it also has special power and significance in crucial situations. A spiritual counselor, for instance, should become adept in its use; first by explaining it and then by praying this prayer with another.

Prayer for inner healing is a form of prayer especially helpful in prayer counseling. It encompasses the healing not only of recent hurts, but past ones as well. Under the guidance and prayer of a spiritual counselor, hurts of various periods of one's life are allowed to surface and are then placed on Christ in the growth center. At the same time, the spiritual counselor prays with the person as the two of them offer a prayer of blessing for the offenders.

Although the need for healing is universal, it is particularly important for those who want to mature yet have festering wounds and deep-seated resentments which impede the maturing process. While praying with a spiritual counselor, there is no need for the individual to reveal confidences he or she does not feel inclined to give. What is allowed to surface is between the individual and the Lord. The following steps may prove helpful in a ministry of spiritual counseling combined with prayer.

1. Begin by praying with the person to the Holy Spirit thanking him for the healing of past wounds and for the gifts of his love, peace, and joy. If the person wishes gently place your hand on his or her shoulder. Pray with the person for the healing of hurts or trauma experienced during pregnancy and early childhood about which the person knows nothing.

2. Next, allow the hurts of later childhood to surface. Then pray to the Holy Spirit to heal these hurts and say a prayer for the persons who inflicted them. Do the same for successive stages of adolescence, early adulthood, and later adulthood. Generally calling to mind persons likely to have inflicted these hurts could prove helpful.

3. Finally, end with a prayer of thanksgiving for the blessings received. Yielding to the Holy Spirit's action during this prayer brings about internal release and healing. The healing which occurs will be maintained to the degree that the person concerned lives a life of prayer and continues to invoke the prayer of blessing on others. An openness to the Holy Spirit will

allow an inflow of his love, peace, and joy to become constant.

It should be noted that spiritual gifts grow through use. The gift of spiritual healing and being used by the Holy Spirit as a channel of his peace and joy to others is strengthened as we invoke his name and call him to assist us. It is in giving that we receive. The time to start is now.

It should be noted here that a psychologist can effect partial relief by encouraging a hate syndrome to surface. But it takes the love of the indwelling Holy Spirit to heal the deeper wound, and this love can be activated through prayer ministry with a prayer counselor.

Again, a form of spiritual healing which has centuries of Christian practice behind it is the use of the Doxology in order to dispel the powers of darkness, relieve oppression, and bring a person into an experience of God's love and joy. Here I am also reminded of that beautiful prayer in the Catholic Mass for Christmas Eve. "When He came to us as man, the Son of God scattered the darkness of this world and filled this holy night with His Glory. May the God of infinite goodness scatter the darkness of sin and brighten your hearts with holiness."

Encouraging a deep prayer life and using prayer in relation to counseling is essential. Prayer in itself can be the most effective ministry open to Christians today—prayer by yourself, with a prayer partner or in a prayer group. This is true because in the first place, in a very unique way, prayer is service, and like service it is rooted in love. Moreover, prayer can be addressed not to one or several, but to all needs whether physical, spiritual, social, or personal.

Prayer ministry is at the very heart of social renewal, since like a city power plant it furnishes energy for those in need, be they leaders or leaveners of our society. In the context of agape love, mature prayer can become a centered, authentic, unifying force in society. It is a means of uniting us to the vine and of bearing fruit in abundance. Lastly, it offers a special kind of ministry open to all, regardless of talents or circumstances.

Chapter XV
Ministry for Maturity

The most neglected Christians in our communities today are those who have the greatest potential for revitalizing the church. These are the Christians in quest of depth. Regardless of age, education, cultural background, occupation, or life situation, they search for buried treasures and are hungry and thirsty for the kingdom of God. According to Gallup, among these are six in ten of the unchurched and one half of the churched who say that the church is too concerned with organizational, as opposed to spiritual, aspects of religion. These Christians are not the benchwarmers still content with bingo or potlucks. These are vital people both inside and outside the church who require a new form of evangelism, one that fosters maturity. Maturity is our common Christian responsibility, and it calls for a new ministry, a ministry for maturity. This *new* form of evangelism dedicated to fostering maturity differs from the proclamation of the message to the many, the broadside sowing of the seed, and is devoted rather to the instruction and nurturing of the new Christian who has experienced Christ. It is the frequent watering of the plant the day after we find Christ. It is an enabling ministry which calls for the same zeal as the evangelical proclamation of the good news. It requires the wisdom of the Holy Spirit within to enable us to minister to persons where they are now and to point to where they might go. It is a personal ministry to unique persons with unique needs, which involves instruction, counseling, and supportive prayer as we share Christ's glory with one another (1 Thess. 2:4).

For those who foster maturity, the message of Pentecost has not only been grasped intellectually, but experientially. They realize that the mystery of Christ can only be imparted to others by those who have experienced him in a living, loving, personal relationship themselves. This ministry starts with an understanding of the goal of Christianity: maturing in Christ (Eph. 4:13). We must have the inner wisdom which the Holy Spirit gives along with his indwelling presence for any degree of effectiveness.

As Christians today living in an upset world, we must recognize our common responsibility to foster maturity, particularly on the level of Christian consciousness. The already successful collaboration among theologians in the charismatic renewal needs to extend far beyond this movement. Moreover, for the sake of improved communication and greater effectiveness on the pastoral level, there is an urgent need for theologians to clear up their terminologies in the area of Christian consciousness. As already indicated, our understandings are similar, yet the way we express ourselves keeps us poles apart. There is also an immediate need for Christians to combine their efforts to monitor some of the pseudo-psychic religious groups using Christian terminologies. These groups are picking up some of our unsuspecting stray sheep! In general, our zeal in a united effort should be to "put all things to the test and to keep what is good."

While fostering maturity among Christians, on the way to glory, we can become instruments of social renewal. How can we become more effective instruments of the Holy Spirit in renewing the face of the earth? In the past, we have allowed our evangelical zeal to be limited to spiritual infants. But today the demand is for strong and perfect Christians reaching to the full stature of Christ. Hopefully, this book will help many in a personal way to understand and nurture spiritual maturity in their own lives and enable them to foster it in the lives of others. Generally speaking, a ministry for maturity requires that there be data on hand. Often, churches decide, without facts, to move in a given direction on the basis of prayer; others on the basis of facts without prayer. A responsible ministry calls for both. Using factual data from survey research, in a process of creative decision-making with spiritual discernment, as described earlier, should enable church leaders to proceed with clarity and certainty in planning a ministry for maturity.

As a case in point, such an approach should challenge the Evangelicals who are looking today for new approaches to ministry among those who have initially committed their lives to Christ, the churched as well as the unchurched. In a recent study of the unchurched American, George Gallup came up with figures which show that 40 percent of the unchurched have committed their lives to Christ, 45 percent pray frequently, and 10 percent are involved in popular meditation groups. Those committed to a ministry for maturity will find many and varied opportunities to foster a deeper understanding of the growing relationship of communion with Christ in their growth center through counseling with prayer. They will have a special ministry to those who will only come to Christianity through the entrance of transcendence; to those unchurched who according to recent studies will return when they find someone closely connected with the church who will show some personal concern as well as inspire them to deepen their relationship with Christ. Paul says:

> Since you have accepted Christ Jesus as Lord live in union with him. Keep your roots deep in him, build your lives on him, and become ever stronger in your faith as you were taught. And be filled with thanksgiving. (Col. 2:6)

Survey research can indeed become an essential aspect of a ministry for maturity. New areas for interfaith research to consider could deal with the general question as to how the church can have greater spiritual meaning. Many of these people are searching for depth in oriental sects. How best can the wisdom and depth of Christianity be presented to them, particularly those Ph.D.'s with a third-grade knowledge of

Christianity? Should we not evangelize in greater depth, drawing on the more profound passages found in John's Gospel? Was not John the Evangelist also a mystic? We need to discover ways to attract Christians to a deeper understanding of Christianity. What are the obstacles, what are the possibilities for the future?

Looking at the situation factually, a recent survey of Gallup shows that 88 percent of American teen-agers, Protestant and Catholic, say they have had an "experience of the presence of God." It would appear that young people know what the essence of Christian consciousness is all about and understand by experience the heart of the Christian message. Our responsibility is to study the situation and to discover what this valuable data may be saying to Christian churches. We need to probe further to discover whether the nature of our ministry is nurturing.

Indeed these teen-agers may have had a genuine focal awakening, in which case the maturing process in a relational faith has begun. To them, Christian consciousness is already something real. Perhaps, response research, i.e., the designing and pretesting of alternate models to meet specific needs, might lead to the replacing of a coach with a spiritual guidance counselor or to having meditation days in the woods, the mountains, and on the seashore. This form of response research might also reveal that it is no longer necessary for the church to duplicate the recreation park. A youth interested in ashrams wrote on a questionnaire: "I left the church when it became 'relevant!' " Perhaps the youth minister of the future should be a graduate of the Ecumenical Charismatic Institute in Melodyland, California, or one willing to don a saffron garb rather than a motorcycle helmet while teaching the Jesus Prayer. Is it an accident that the largest percentage of young people involved in the Hare Krishna Movement have come from mainline denominations —Roman Catholics, Presbyterians, Methodists, Episcopalians? What does this tell us? A mother whose two daughters are in the Divine Light Mission remarked to me in despair, "I could not suggest an alternative."

Response research holds endless possibilities for exploring appropriate and workable approaches to fostering maturity and a ministry for maturity:

a) for those in public life who complain they receive plenty of pressure but little supportive ministry or pastoral care.

b) for those involved in T.M. and other popular meditation groups who are searching for guidance in Christian meditation.

c) for those who are disillusioned with the church community and say it has lost its spiritual meaning.

d) for parents seeking ways to develop spiritual maturity in the home.

e) for special categories of persons with special needs such as retirees and divorcees.

f) for those who could perform remarkable services in phone ministries supportive of one another, such as the elderly, the handicapped, or incurables.

g) for veterans confined in hospitals, for prisoners who can develop peer group ministries.

h) for those who are having spiritual growing pains and are seeking a more effective outreach to others.

It is in regard to this last point that the need for response research becomes increasingly apparent. There is a crying need today to probe the best way churches can respond to those who are ready for a prayer-in-action approach to life and who are awaiting a ministry for maturity. A new volunteerism is in the air which requires careful study and analysis. It raises some serious questions about our approach to ministry in general. For instance, do we give more attention in recruiting to talent rather than commitment? (As noted earlier, although Peter was a "lousy" fisherman and "perspired a lot," he did love Christ. And the condition of his assignment was: "Peter, lovest thou me? Feed my lambs, feed my sheep.")

As a case in point of fostering a ministry for maturity,

a questionnaire might be designed on this new volunteerism as it relates to maturity for ministry and a ministry for maturity to sort out the best approaches to spiritual formation, as well as the affirmation of the individual's special abilities for service. The key emphasis should highlight the importance of coordination vs. organization and how we can best identify those persons aspiring to spiritual maturity and a prayer-in-action ministry. Where are they? How can we bring Christians with a sense of dedication together in terms of existing needs? How can we relate persons with complimentary talents and mutual interests in a team effort directed to a common cause? What are the possibilities among churches for collaborative effort in fostering a ministry for maturity?

In view of the above, the preparing of a research effort should begin by reviewing church history. Not too many seem aware of the fact that in the early church committed volunteers were in the middle-age bracket. The trend was not in the direction of recruiting youth. Adaptation of existing programs, such as the Peace Corps, should be examined to discover what can be learned from their experience. On the basis of wisdom gained over the years, old approaches can be born again. We need to put all things to the test and keep what is good.

A major response research project to develop new models for volunteerism as related to a ministry for maturity is in order. Its first assumption would be that all involved would be striving for maturity built on authentic vertical and horizontal love relationships as prayer in action became a way of life. What is important to bear in mind, however, is that survey research can merely supplement and confirm the wisdom and experience of Christians throughout the centuries guided by the Holy Spirit. If a ministry for maturity is to succeed at all it must be rooted in prayer and the importance of "metanoia," a conversion and deep change of heart in which we die on a certain level in order to find ourselves alive on another more spiritual level. Such a ministry will be mindful of the fact that the New Testament is highly critical of a faith that refuses to mature. "By this time you ought to be teachers, but instead you need someone to teach you all over again the first principles of God's will" (Heb. 5:12). Maturity for ministry must be marked by presence, peace, and power!

The Holy Spirit as the Minister of Maturity

Jesus realized the great need for a ministry for maturity, and he assured us that we would not lack his support. The washing of the feet of the apostles was merely symbolic of the more important ministry of the cleansing, healing, and unifying of our spirits through the Advocate he promised to send. It was at this very time that Jesus assured us that the Holy Spirit would dwell in us and personally minister to us. He said that as we experienced a deepening relationship with him there would be an overflowing of love toward others in an activated faith.

A ministry for maturity is based on the principle that "we can be made a holy people by his Spirit" (1 Pet. 1:2) as we continue to grow and to help each other in the grace and knowledge of our Lord and Savior Jesus Christ "until the day dawns and the light of the morning star [Christ] rises in our hearts" (2 Pet. 1:19). Scripture promises that "after we have suffered a little while, the God of all grace, who has called you to his eternal glory in Christ, will himself restore, establish, and strengthen you" (1 Pet. 5:10).

My hope is that many Christians will experience a call to a ministry for maturity in one form or another whether through instruction, counseling, prayer, or research. A call to such a ministry begins with the experience of the love of a personal God who first loved us (1 John 4:10). The beginning is like the call of the Good Shepherd, a response is created in us, an interior movement, a love on a new level of consciousness, a focal awakening, that grows in depth from loving communication to communion as we reach out to others. The more we become involved in a ministry for maturity, the more we will begin to understand how the Risen Christ has been given us to share with one another. We will be inspired by Christians who have already incarnated the love of Christ in their lives on the level of a Christian consciousness which has expanded into prayer in action. With such fertile soil, we will witness a blossoming of a new vitality in Christianity far exceeding anything known to the ancient religions, because we will have assumed our common responsibility for Christian maturity.

In conclusion, I might add, that love as the bond of unity between time and eternity needs serious consideration in the Christian framework by those today who are interested in proving life after death. Even now on earth God wishes us to relate to one another through a love activated by prayer, so that in heaven we will love each other with a love of gratefulness and a love which has its source in Christ. The chagrin of Augustine, "too late have I loved thee," was very real. Therese of Lisieux, however, had an answer for him. She insisted she would spend her heaven in assisting others to love God as she loved him. She saw her limited ministry on earth in terms of a ministry for maturity in eternity.

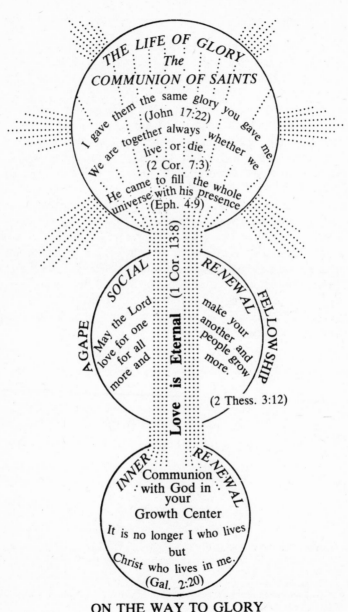

THE LIFE OF GLORY
The
COMMUNION OF SAINTS

I gave them the same glory you gave me
(John 17:22)
We are together always whether we
live or die.
(2 Cor. 7:3)
He came to fill the whole
universe with his presence
(Eph. 4:9)

SOCIAL RENEWAL
AGAPE FELLOWSHIP
Love is Eternal (1 Cor. 13:8)

May the Lord
love for one
for all
more and

make your
another and
people grow
more.

(2 Thess. 3:12)

INNER RENEWAL
Communion
with God in
your
Growth Center
It is no longer I who lives
but
Christ who lives in me.
(Gal. 2:20)

ON THE WAY TO GLORY

Notes

CHAPTER ONE
Put All Things to the Test

1. *Christian Ministry* (November 15, 1975).

CHAPTER TWO
Christian Maturity: The Call of All

1. Sister Mary Melannie, S.N.D., "Personality Pete," *National Catholic Reporter* (December 17, 1976).
2. John Mackay, *Christian Reality and Appearance* (Richmond: John Knox Press, 1969), pp. 24–25.
3. H. A. Reinhold, ed., *The Soul Afire, Revelations of the Mystics* (Garden City, N.Y.; Doubleday Image Books, 1973), p. 36–37.

CHAPTER THREE
Probing Our Roots

1. Thomas Merton, *The New Man* (New York: Farrar, Straus & Giroux, 1963), p. 11.
2. Merton, "The Life That Unifies," *Sisters Today* 42, No. 2.
3. Albert E. Day, *The Captivating Presence* (Nashville, 1971), pp. 10–25.
4. G. M. Behler, *The Last Discourse of Jesus* (Baltimore: Helicon Press, 1965), p. 104.
5. Brother Lawrence, *The Practice of the Presence of God* (Old Tappan, N.J.: Fleming H. Revell, 1958), p. 11.
6. A Monk of the Orthodox Church, *Orthodox Spirituality* (London: Fellowship of St. Alban and Sergius, 1968), p. 95.

CHAPTER FOUR
From Communication to Communion with God

1. John of the Cross, *The Living Flame of Love* in the Collected Works of John of the Cross, ed., K. Kavanaugh and C. Rodriguez (Washington: I.C.S. Publications, 1973), p. 586.
2. *Ibid.*
3. William Johnston, *The Mysticism of the Cloud of Unknowing* (St. Meinrad, Ind.: Abbey Press, 1975), p. 155.

4. Yves Ranguin, *How to Pray Today* (St. Meinrad, Ind.: Abbey Press, 1974), p. 121.
5. George Maloney, S.J., *How to Know and Evaluate the Occult* (Albany, N.Y.: Crux Clarity).
6. John of the Cross, *Living Flame,* p. 585.
7. A Monk, *Orthodox Spirituality,* p. 98.
8. Simone Weil, *First and Last Notebooks,* Richard Rees, ed. (London: Oxford University Press, 1970), p. 288.

CHAPTER FIVE
Agape Consciousness

1. Mackay, *Christian Reality,* p. 53.
2. Pierre Teilhard de Chardin, *The Future of Man* (New York: Harper & Row, 1959), p. 286.

CHAPTER SIX
From Communication to Communion in Fellowship

1. Dietrich Bonhoeffer, *The Communion of Saints* (New York: Harper & Row, 1960), p. 147.
2. Thomas Kelly, *A Testament of Devotion* (New York: Harper & Row, 1941), p. 10.

CHAPTER SEVEN
An Activated Faith: Prayer in Action

1. Pierre Teilhard de Chardin, *The Divine Milieu* (New York: Harper & Row, 1960), p. 66.
2. Teresa of Avila, *The Interior Castle,* trans., Allison Peers (Garden City, N.Y.: Doubleday Image Books, 1944) p. 228.
3. Miriam Murphy, "Mainline Charismatic," *Christian Century* (September 27, 1972).

CHAPTER EIGHT
Breathing a Prayer

1. Kelly, *Testament,* pp. 55, 120.
2. John of the Cross, *The Spiritual Canticle* in Collected Works, p. 481.
3. *Ibid.*

CHAPTER NINE
From Inner Renewal to Social Renewal

1. Murphy, "Mainline Charismatic."
2. Thomas Carlisle, "Subpoena," *Christian Century* (February 10, 1971).
3. Kelly, *Testament.*

CHAPTER TEN
A Sustaining Life-Style

1. Teresa of Avila, *Interior Castle*, ch. 15.
2. John of the Cross, *Spiritual Canticle*, p. 544.
3. John of the Cross, *Living Flame*, p. 583.
4. John of the Cross, *Ascent of Mt. Carmel*, p. 149.
5. Simone Weil, *Waiting for God* (London: Broadway House, 1950), p. 93.

CHAPTER ELEVEN
The Prayer of Referral

1. Simone Weil, *Gateway to God* (London: Fontane, 1974), p. 176.
2. *Ibid.*, p. 176.
3. Brother Lawrence, *Presence of God*, p. 48.
4. Reinhold, ed., *Soul Afire*, p. 426.
5. Pierre Teilhard de Chardin, *Building the Earth* (Denville, N.J.: Dimension Press, 1965), p. 111.

CHAPTER TWELVE
A New Look at the Jesus Prayer

1. F. C. Happhold, *Prayer and Meditation* (New Orleans: Pelican Press, 1971), pp. 127–37.
2. A Monk of the Orthodox Church, *On the Invocation of the Name of Jesus* (London: Fellowship of St. Alban and Sergius, 1969), pp. 1–25.

CHAPTER THIRTEEN
A Prayer of Forgiveness and Blessing

1. William Johnston, *Silent Music* (New York: Harper & Row, 1974), p. 120.
2. *Ibid.*
3. Evelyn Underhill, *An Anthology of the Love of God* (London: A. R. Mowbray 1953), p. 190.

CHAPTER FOURTEEN
Maturity for Ministry

1. Simon Tugwell, *Have You Received the Spirit?* (Paramus, N.J.: Paulist/Newman, 1972), p. 94.

Bibliography

RECOMMENDED READING

Aumann, Jordan, O.P., Thomas Hopko, Donald Bloesch. *Christian Spirituality East and West.* Chicago: Priory Press, 1967.

Cox, Harvey. *Turning East: The Promise and Peril of the New Orientalism.* New York: Simon & Schuster, 1977.

Dechanet, J. M. *Christian Yoga.* Christian Classics, 1976.

Greeley, Andrew. *Ecstasy.* Englewood Cliffs, N.J.: Prentice-Hall, 1974.

Happhold, F. C. *Mysticism: A Study and an Anthology.* Baltimore: Penguin Books, 1963.

———. *The Journey Inwards.* London: Darton, Longman & Todd, 1968.

———. *Prayer and Meditation.* Baltimore: Penguin Books, 1971.

Harkness, Georgia. *Mysticism: Its Meaning and Message.* Nashville: Abingdon, 1973.

Brother Lawrence. *The Practice of the Presence of God.* Old Tappan, N.J.: Fleming H. Revell, 1958.

John of the Cross. *The Dark Night of the Soul.* Garden City, N.Y.: Doubleday Image Books.

———. *The Ascent of Mt. Carmel. Ibid.*

———. *The Living Flame of Love. Ibid.*

Johnston, William. *Silent Music.* New York: Harper & Row, 1974.

———. *The Still Point.* Bronx: Fordham University Press, 1970.

———. *Christian Zen.* New York: Harper & Row, 1971.

———. *The Mysticism of the Cloud of Unknowing and the Book of Privy Counselling.* Garden City, N.Y.: Doubleday, 1973.

Kelly, Thomas. *Testament of Devotion.* New York: Harper & Row, 1941.

MacNutt, Francis. *Healing.* Notre Dame University Press, 1974.

Maletesta, Edward J., ed. The Religious Experience Series. St. Meinrad, Ind.: Abbey Press. Vol. 1, *Jesus in Christian Devotion and Contemplation;* Vol. 4, *How to Pray Today;* Vol. 5, *Imitating*

Christ; Vol. 6, Paths to Contemplation; Vol. 7, *The Depths of God: The Theology of Contemplation.*

Maloney, George. *The Breath of the Mystic,* Denville, N. J. Dimension Books, 1974.

———. *Inward Stillness, Ibid.,* 1975.

———. *Listen Prophets, Ibid.,* 1974.

———. *Mary the Womb of God, Ibid.;* 1976.

Merton, Thomas. *Contemplative Prayer.* Garden City, N.Y.: Doubleday Image Books, 1971.

———. *Contemplation in a World of Action.* Garden City, N.Y.: Doubleday, 1971.

———. *Contemplative Prayer.* New York: Herder and Herder, 1969.

———. *Mystics and Zen Masters.* New York: Farrar, Straus & Giroux, 1969.

———. *New Seeds of Contemplation.* New York: New Directions, 1961.

———. *Seeds of Contemplation. Ibid.,* 1949.

———. *Seven Story Mountain.* New York: New American Library, 1952.

———. *Spiritual Direction and Meditation.* Collegeville, Minn.: Liturgical Press, 1960.

A Monk of the Orthodox Church. *The Prayer of Jesus.* Desclee Co., 1967.

Nouwen, Henri. *Outreach.* Garden City, N.Y.: Doubleday, 1974.

Otto, Rudolph. *Mysticism East and West.* Cleveland: World Publishing Co., 1970.

Peers, Allison. *The Complete Works of St. Teresa of Jesus.* N.Y.: Sheed & Ward, 1950.

Poslusney, Venard. *The Art of Aspiration.* Locust Valley, N.Y.: Living Flame Press, 1974.

Reinhold, H. A., ed. *The Soul Afire: Revelations of the Mystics,* Garden City, N.Y.: Doubleday Image Books, 1973.

Spencer, Sidney. *Mysticism in World Religions.* Baltimore: Pelican Books, 1963.

Stace, W. T. *The Teaching of the Mystics.* Mentor Books.

Teresa of Avila. *Autobiography.* Garden City, N.Y.: Doubleday Image Books, 1973.

———. *The Interior Castle. Ibid.,* 1944.

Tugwell, Simon. *Have You Received the Spirit?* Paramus, N.J.: Paulist/Newman Press, 1976.

Weil, Simone. *Waiting for God.* New York: Harper & Row.

White, John, ed. *The Highest State of Consciousness.* Garden City, N.Y.: Doubleday Anchor Books.

————. *Frontiers of Consciousness: The Meeting Ground Between Inner and Outer Reality.* N.Y.: Julian Press, 1974.

Williams, Rodman. *The Era of the Holy Spirit.* Plainfield, N.J.: Logos International.

Zuzuka, D. T. An *Introduction to Zen Buddhism.* Rider.